Winning the Second Half

Thriving through midlife and beyond

Matt Elliott & Susan Pearse

First published by Busybird Publishing 2025

Copyright © 2025 Matt Elliott & Susan Pearse

ISBN
Print: 978-1-923501-04-1
Ebook: 978-1-923501-05-8

This work is copyright. Apart from any use permitted under the *Copyright Act 1968*, no part of this publication may be reproduced, stored in a retrieval system or transmitted in any form or by any means, electronic, mechanical, photocopying, recording or otherwise, without the prior written permission of Matt Elliott & Susan Pearse.

All rights reserved. No part of this book may be reproduced by any mechanical, photographic, or electronic process, or in the form of a phonographic recording; nor may it be stored in a retrieval system, transmitted, or otherwise be copied for public or private use—other than for "fair use" as brief quotations embodied in articles and reviews—without prior written permission of the publisher.

The authors of this book do not dispense medical advice or prescribe the use of any technique as a form of treatment for physical, emotional, or medical problems without the advice of a physician, either directly or indirectly. The intent of the authors is only to offer information of a general nature to help you in your quest for emotional and spiritual well-being. In the event you use any of the information in this book for yourself, the authors and the publisher assume no responsibility for your actions.

Front Cover concept: Imprint Co Pty Ltd

Layout and typesetting: Busybird Publishing

Busybird Publishing
2/118 Para Road
Montmorency, Victoria
Australia 3094
www.busybird.com.au

Other Books and Resources

Susan Pearse

- **Wired For Life** – *Retrain Your Brain and Thrive (with Martina Sheehan) Hay House Australia*
- **One Moment Please** – *It's Time To Pay Attention (with Martina Sheehan) Hay House Australia*
- **Do Less Be More** – *Ban Busy and Make Space For What Matters (with Martina Sheehan) Hay House Australia*
- **Spiritually Loose** – *Uncover the Path to Your Divine Life, Hay House Australia*

Matt Elliott

- **The Change Room** – *Play The Game of Life*
- The Change Room Podcast

Matt's Dedication

The real reason behind writing this book and wanting to thrive in life while still proudly holding onto a paper birth certificate is simple; I wanted more time and unforgettable experiences with my beautiful daughters.

So, to Mia, Lucy, Claire, and Katie this book is for you, now and forever, just like my love for each of you. You are my greatest motivation and my daily reminder of what truly matters.

To my amazing grandkids Isla, Jesse, Hunter, and Sonny you little legends are the spark behind Winning the Second Half. Your energy, curiosity, and joy light the path ahead.

Susan's Dedication

To Mum and Dad, your lives are a shining example of what it means to truly thrive in the second half of life. In your 80s, you continue to inspire me with your energy, bright minds, and unwavering spirit.

If I carry even half the vitality you embody, I will consider myself fortunate. The legacy you've created reaches far beyond me, it lives on in my children, Holly and Jack, who are growing up with the gift of your example. Thank you for being my greatest inspiration for an amazing second half.

Acknowledgements

To the many people who shared in deep, thoughtful conversations that sparked ideas woven throughout these pages; Martina, Phil, Karla, Kerri, Rachel, Shannon, Narelle, Charlie, Peter, and countless others thank you. Your insights, questions, and perspectives were invaluable in shaping the heart of this book. To Leon, your expert mentorship and joyous wit made this journey both enlightening and fun!

Susan

To my brothers-in-arms: Brian (NFL sidekick), and Leon (NRL Pal) thank you for the laughs, the deep chats, and for being part of this wild ride. Every chapter carries a bit of your spirit, you've all left fingerprints on every page.
Let's keep showing up, having fun, and playing hard in the second half,

Matt

A Shoutout to the Dream Team

To our amazing writing and editing trio Martina Sheehan, Maggie Hamilton and Margie Tubbs what a ride it's been! Your guidance, wisdom, and unwavering support have been the invisible threads holding this book together. You've helped shape not just the words, but the heart of this project.

We are endlessly grateful for your belief in this book and now that it's here, we hope you feel as proud as we do. This isn't just a book, it's a spark for change and a guide for thriving for everyone navigating the Second Half.

Thank you for helping us bring it to life.

Testimonial

When we were invited to read Winning the Second Half, we didn't quite realise how much it would speak to both of us, individually and as a couple. What Susan and Matt have created is far more than a book about longevity; it's a powerful invitation to redefine the way we see ourselves as we move through life's so-called "second half."

For Anthony, whose identity for so long was wrapped around physical performance and peak fitness, this book offered a fresh lens on what strength truly means. It challenged some long-held subconscious beliefs about aging, and beliefs we didn't even realise we had, giving a clear, inspiring blueprint for thriving beyond the boundaries society often sets at 40.

For Terry, it was the emotional and spiritual threads of the book that resonated deeply. Susan and Matt have a beautiful way of guiding you back to your own power, purpose and presence. The way they frame aging, not as a decline but as a deepening has transformed how we look at this chapter of our lives, not with fear, but with fire and fun.

What stood out most was the reminder that reinvention isn't just possible, it's necessary. The second half of life, as Susan and Matt show us, isn't about slowing down or playing it safe. It's about elevating your relationships, finding new energy, and leaning into joy, clarity and contribution with open arms.

This book has shifted how we plan, how we live, and how we love. We're grateful for it and excited for everyone who picks it up to experience the same powerful shift.

With love and gratitude,

Anthony Minichiello
Voted World's Best Rugby League Player
&
Terry Biviano
Designer and Reality TV Star

Contents

Other Books and Resources	i
Acknowledgements	v
Testimonial	vii
Foreword	xi

Section 1 - The Midlife Evolution — 1
- Chapter 1 - The Wake-up Call — 3
- Chapter 2 - Life in the Afternoon — 7
- Chapter 3 - Moving to Your Own Beat — 13
- Chapter 4 - Changing Demographics — 22
- Chapter 5 - Mindset Matters — 31

Section 2 - Secret Women's Business — 37
- Chapter 6 - The Female Narrative — 39
- Chapter 7 - A New Narrative — 44
- Chapter 8 - Creative Woman, Nurturing Woman, Wise Woman — 48
- Chapter 9 - Stop. Rest. Re-energise. Celebrate. — 53
- Chapter 10 - The Menopause Mystery — 57
- Chapter 11 - Elevate to the Top of the Pile — 64

Section 3 - Unspoken Men's Business — 73
- Chapter 12 - Men's Talk — 75
- Chapter 13 - Redefining Outdated Norms — 80
- Chapter 14 - Rules for Life — 87
- Chapter 15 - The Power of Self-Awareness — 93
- Chapter 16 - Busting Myths — 98

Section 4 - Let's Get Physical — 109
- Chapter 17 - Decomplicating the Physical — 111
- Chapter 18 - Diet — 119
- Chapter 19 - Exercise — 128
- Chapter 20 - Sleep to Thrive — 143
- Chapter 21 - Breathing for Life — 150
- Chapter 22 - Final Words — 154

Section 5 - Happy and Healthy Mind — 157
Chapter 23 - Midlife Mind Motivation — 158
Chapter 24 - The Challenge of AI — 167
Chapter 25 - Hanging Out in Your Mind Garden — 171
Chapter 26 - The Foundation – Self-Awareness — 175
Chapter 27 - Mindfulness Practice — 180
Chapter 28 - Mindset Practice — 195
Chapter 29 - Mind Skill Practice — 217

Section 6 - Master Your Emotions — 223
Chapter 30 - Riding the Emotional Wave — 225
Chapter 31 - Unresolved Emotions — 230
Chapter 32 - Building Emotional Capacities — 239
Chapter 33 - The Emotional Blueprint — 243
Chapter 34 - Emotional Resilience — 249
Chapter 35 - Emotions and Women — 254

Section 7 - Connection through Spirituality — 269
Chapter 36 - Midlife Spiritual Awakenings — 271
Chapter 37 - Spiritual Connection — 279
Chapter 38 - Connecting with Your True Self — 282
Chapter 39 - Connecting to Others — 292
Chapter 40 - Connecting to a Higher Force — 301

Section 8 - Embracing the Full-Time Hooter — 317
Final Words for Now — 319
Appendix 1 - Common symptoms of menopause — 325
References — 327
About the Authors — 331

Foreword

What you are seeking is also seeking you.

Rumi

What we experience is never simply the world as it is, but the world as we are. Over time, that lens deepens when we let experiences sharpen our awareness. What once felt urgent begins to feel a bit more optional, and what was out of reach becomes clearer and a touch more grounded.

Winning the Second Half is not about reclaiming youth, resisting change, or compensating for what time has taken away, but recognising what time has given you. This book reminds us to cultivate greater self-knowledge, a perspective on life, and emotional depth.

Post 40 and even more so when you start 50-plus laps of the sun, the opportunity is no longer about accumulation but finding your alignment. Living with clarity, energy, and meaning that are internally sourced rather than externally driven.

This book reflects that understanding, and rather than offering strategies to hustle or reinvent yourself, Winning the Second Half invites you to return to what already exists within you. It challenges the belief that fulfilment, vitality, or relevance must be chased or earned, instead suggesting that many of the qualities we seek, like happiness, resilience or contribution, are found by removing what no longer serves us in life.

In my own life, I have seen this repeatedly, when I expanded my perspective, released outdated narratives, and reconnected to myself, new possibilities emerged, and these were often more meaningful than those imagined earlier in life.

The second half is not a narrowing of options, and this book reminded me that it was about the widening of choice. Take the invitation to step into that space with intention, awareness, and confidence.

Mary Gourley
Google Lead Executive,
Agentic Workplace Transformation – JAPAC.

Section 1
The Midlife Evolution

Chapter 1

The Wake-up Call

Susan and I had hardly begun our conversation when she hit me with an unexpected admission: "Matt, I've got an outfit in my wardrobe that's reserved just for funerals. Lately, it's been out way more than I'd like."

"Whoa! Hang on a tick, Susan," I responded, shifting uncomfortably in my seat. "This book is about how to win the second half of life, not how to blow the full-time hooter!"

"Well said," Susan laughed, "and while I've never particularly been into sport, I'm actually enjoying some of your terminology. Let me 'play on' with my point, before you go 'kicking another goal'. You can't win the second half if you don't have a game plan," insisted Susan. "When you're in the home stretch, the last thing you want to do is drop the ball, because this is the Grand Final. When the full-time hooter blows and the game ends, life stops. You've got to understand the end game, if you want to bring your best game."

Geez. I was struck by an unfamiliar sense of vulnerability as her words hit me. "I wish I could argue with you Susan, but you're right. I guess, like most guys, my first response is to be in denial about it. My subconscious is screaming: *You don't have time to die, mate! You have too much stuff to do!*"

Did I spy a little pity in Susan's eye, or maybe it was just a playful twinkle. "Funerals are definitely a wake-up call; but honestly, Matt, I get a shock every day when I look in the mirror and see a new grey hair, another wrinkle, hands that look well, older. Sometimes I barely recognise myself. I have to stop and ask, 'Is that really me?' I still remember 18-year-old Susan like it was yesterday."

"Grey?" I retort. "No way – those babies are stainless steel!"

Now Susan definitely had a wry look on her face. "Matt, that delusion you mentioned earlier, it's time to park it."

She was right. In fact, it's great advice for all of us. Delusion and denial only hold us back from living a full life. To have a great second half, we all need a game plan and a good reality check. That's what we hope to offer in this book.

Matt: I'll be honest, between my eyesight heading south and the space between my grey hairs getting bigger, I might need to accept that I'm ageing. There are days when this freaks me out, leaving me feeling a bit vulnerable.

Susan: Exactly! My eyes aren't what they used to be. Neither is my body. I remember when I could go out drinking on a work night, get an hour of sleep, and still be fine the next day. Now? One glass of wine and my brain feels foggy for hours. Not to mention all my menopause symptoms. These changes do leave us a bit vulnerable, but perhaps they're just a call for us to take better care of ourselves.

Matt: Midlife bodies don't let you get away with the things you did when you were younger. But maybe that's a good thing; our bodies are telling us to shape up.

Susan: And funerals do that for me too. They remind me how fragile life is, and they push me to take better care of myself. They also give me a good dose of:

- *Take the risk!*
- *Make the connection.*
- *If not now, when?*
- *Just do it!*

Matt: Now that's what excites me about the second half! Sure, I won't be playing professional rugby again, but there's an infinite list of things I can do which might be even more exciting than anything I did when I was younger. Welcome to the second half of life, where the game is still on and the best plays might be yet to come!

Susan: I agree Matt, and I've already started doing some of those exciting new things. But before we dive into all that, have you noticed that most people don't like it when you tell them they're in their second half? I was at dinner with a couple chatting about our ideas for this book, and the 52-year-old wife exclaimed, "I'm not in my second half!" It was pretty clear from the pitch of her voice that she had taken offence. "Well, if you think you're going to live to 104 you are!" her husband chimed in. I must admit I was amused by how shocked she looked as his words sank in.

Matt: Yes, I get that a lot. I don't think many people have considered the simple arithmetic. In Australia, where you and I both live, the life expectancy for men is 81.1 years and for women it's 85.1 years. There's only one documented case of someone living beyond 120 years anywhere in the world, so even if you're an extreme optimist who hopes to be a centenarian, I feel pretty safe saying that most of us reach the halfway point of our lives in our 40s, and in some countries it's much lower. After that, you're in the second half.

Although there's lots of talk about longevity and the potential for science to discover ways to extend our lifespan by a significant number of years, until that's a reality, I am more interested in extending my healthspan and making the most of the years I have.

That's what this book's all about. Winning in the second half means thriving all the way into your Golden Years, remaining active, vital, engaged, excited and happy. None of that happens by accident. Midlife presents challenges, but it's also full of opportunity. We hope the stories and tips in this book get you thinking deeply about the choices you're making now to set yourself up for a winning second half.

Chapter 2

Life in the Afternoon

The afternoon of life is just as full of meaning as the morning; only, it's meaning and purpose is different.

Carl Jung, Swiss psychiatrist and psychoanalyst

I could see there was a question on Susan's mind. Finally, it surfaced. "Matt, when someone asks you, who's the person, dead or alive, you'd most like to have dinner with, who comes to mind?"

Matt: Well, about 20 names immediately come to mind, but you're restricting me to just one, right?

Susan: Correct, Matt. We're in our second half, so we don't have time to feed everyone.

Matt: Fair call. Honestly, I'd love to say my 10-year-old self, but I'm keeping that one in my back pocket for later in the book. If you really twisted my arm though, I'd have to say Neville Goddard. I'm a massive fan of Wayne Dyer, Esther Hicks and Joe Dispenza; But Neville? He's next level for me. Born in the early 1900s, he completely reframed my understanding of foundational energy and how ancient wisdom has been twisted, misused and, in many ways, forgotten. He made common sense out of the deep, mystical question of "Who am I?" and how we can harness that power for good.

One thing's for sure; this wouldn't be some quick, polite dinner. We'd be sitting down for a 15-course feast, stretching well past midnight. Just to ensure he couldn't escape my curious mind too early, I'd lose my house keys and have to call a locksmith at 9am. "Sorry, mate, looks like you're stuck answering my questions for a few more hours." I know I've waffled on way too much again. Tell me yours, Susan.

Susan: Carl Jung is always the first for me. He was a Swiss psychiatrist and psychoanalyst in the early 1900s, and I came across his work during my university days. He's wise on so many things but I have recently found his writings on ageing. His teachings speak of 3 distinct phases we move through in life:

1. *Morning is youth.*
2. *Lunchtime is midlife.*
3. *Night is old age.*

His analogy of the passage of the sun through the sky from morning to night is a reminder that we are meant to live out the full cycle of human existence. And that's the thing, it's a cycle. Life is not a linear race; it's a constant evolution. We grow, we adapt and we change. We build knowledge and experience, and we convert it to self-awareness and wisdom. Every step of our passage through life presents space for joyful experiences, and none of our life stages are necessarily better than others.

My favourite time of day has always been late afternoon.

There's a peace in the air, the colours in the sky are at their most beautiful, and the anticipation of magic is all around. Imagine if we looked at our second half through the lens of that filter? Personally, I think it's the most special part of the cycle, a time not just to live but to enjoy.

Jung felt that humans struggle with ageing because we don't understand and value cycles, and I think he has a point. In modern society, we have electric lights to avoid the natural cycle of light and dark, and air conditioning that numbs us to the seasons. Modern medicine blunts our body's natural cycles with all sorts of drugs that enable us to alter our sleep patterns, ignore our fluctuating hormones, and even eliminate our hunger pangs. We are left with the idea that cycles should be avoided. Instead, we've been encouraged to strive for consistency, stability and sameness. But what would it look like if we celebrated the graceful release of one phase and welcomed the arrival of another?

Modern theorists have come to similar conclusions. The term 'middlescence' was coined by Barbara Waxman to explain our midlife transition. Like adolescence, it is accompanied by physical, emotional and hormonal changes; it can be a time of confusion and frustration, but also of growth and transformation.

Matt: This is beginning to sound like the description of a midlife crisis!

Susan: But it doesn't have to be. I prefer to think of it as a liminal space, the time in between 2 different states, like the metamorphosis of a caterpillar into a fully formed butterfly. You feel the need to shed some of what you were before, to experiment with what might be possible, and to decide who you want to be for your second half of life on this planet.

And sure, many people find themselves going way off-course during this transition.

We've all heard the stereotype of the old guy with a new red convertible, or the one who trades his wife in for a newer model. And it's just as common for a woman to hit 50 and take a toy boy, or head to Bali and go all *Eat, Pray, Love.*

Matt: The midlife crisis has traditionally been a male thing. Are you saying women go through it too?

I had to let go of nostalgia for the past and instead, celebrate the richness of life ahead.

Susan: It might have traditionally been viewed as an exclusively male condition, but we all go through this transition. The phrase "midlife crisis" was first coined by psychologist Elliot Jacques in the 1960s, when he described it as the period of your life when you "reckon with your mortality". We most commonly associate it with reckless and 'out of character' choices, but reaching an age when you realise half your life is over can result in many different reactions. Sure, it sends some people straight to the Ferrari dealer or cosmetic surgeon, but it triggers a larger portion of people to try to make sense of their life by asking the deep questions:

- *Where am I now?*

- *Is that good enough?*
- *How has my past led to this?*
- *What do I want for my future?*

This is not a crisis; it's an opportunity, an awakening, a call to reinvention! That's exciting – nothing like a crisis about it.

But if you're unprepared for the significance of this midlife transformation, you're more likely to fall into some common traps:

Negative narrative: Your body responds to the stories your mind tells it. If you believe you're on a downhill slope, your body will reflect that belief. Studies show that people with positive self-perceptions about ageing live 7.5 years longer than those who don't maintain such mindsets.[1] There are compelling reasons to take charge of your narrative and set your own mindsets around the second half.

Spinning: If you dive into random action during a major life change with no clear idea of why you're doing it, there's a big risk that nothing you do will satisfy you. The sporty red Ferrari and the new-look clothes won't help answer any deep questions about life, and so they are followed by surfing lessons and a longboard that requires swapping the Ferrari for a big SUV. Then the new younger wife, then more kids, then a second divorce. It brings to mind a quote I've heard, along the lines: *Action without strategy is a nightmare!* People can spin for an awfully long time, and it's going to be painful for them and others in their life.

Denial: Trying to hold onto your first half might sound

---

1 - See References 1.

appealing, but is it? Ignoring the potential for declining health is just one obvious way that people can miss the opportunity to set themselves up for a thriving second half. Our needs change throughout our second half, and unless you are willing to acknowledge those needs and set up the conditions for thriving, you'll get stuck in a limbo where the activities of the first half no longer thrill you, but you've developed no foundation for finding joy in the second half.

Matt: I struggled with those traps. I was dwelling too much on what was once possible, and I had to work hard at focusing on new experiences that brought me joy and purpose. I had to let go of nostalgia for the past and instead, celebrate the richness of life ahead.

Chapter 3

Moving to Your Own Beat

Susan: I'm keen to hear more about what happened to start you down the road of your midlife evolution, Matt.

Matt: Well, a friend in recruitment had encouraged me to apply for a CEO position that matched my skills perfectly. After sending him my curriculum vitae, he surprised me with this advice: "Matt, change your email address, so it doesn't include your birth year." That's the first time I remember thinking I was old.

Susan: So, what did you do?

Matt: The first thing I said to him was, "Seriously?" I thought maybe he was joking. Surely being born in 1964 didn't make me one of the oldies, but he was serious. "Yeah mate, it could really limit your chances when human resources review your CV."

I was surprised how quickly the feelings of self-doubt rushed in. It made me question my relevance and I wondered if I should be slowing down. I began imagining scenarios where people no longer asked me for advice or valued my contributions. I mulled over it for a while, but it didn't take me long to realise that his suggestion didn't mean I'd lost my edge. However, while my perception of myself got a nice little reminder that life isn't about external limitations, I wasn't as optimistic that others would embrace that approach, so I did actually change my email address.

Susan: It's unfortunate that age triggers these biases, particularly in the workplace. There are so many examples of people doing amazing things in their second half. There is still so much ahead of us all, and it is never too late to start.

Consider these examples:

- ✓ Toni Morrison – she wrote her first novel at 40, won her Pulitzer Prize at 56 and her Nobel Prize at 62.

- ✓ Charles Darwin – he was 50 years old when he published his world-changing book, *On the Origin of the Species.*

- ✓ Vera Wang – the renowned fashion designer must have been doing this forever, right? Wrong. She began her design career at age 40.

- ✓ Henry Ford – he created the revolutionary Model T car at 45 years of age.

- ✓ Ray Kroc and Colonel Sanders – they won't make it into our nutrition section, but it cannot be disputed that they created some of the world's biggest empires. Ray Kroc was 50 when he bought his first McDonalds, and Colonel Sanders was 65 when he established the KFC chain.

- ✓ Julia Child – the celebrity chef wrote her first cookbook at 50, which launched her successful career.

They prove it's never too late for the type of success we usually attribute to the young. But I'm even more encouraged by the stories of ordinary people who prove that later life is a hotbed of creativity, inspiration and passion or just pure, simple contentment. We probably all know someone who ran their first marathon in their 50s, or picked up a guitar or a paint brush for the first time later in life.

The truth is, different types of intelligence peak at different phases in our lives. Fluid Intelligence, our ability to think quickly and recall information, peaks in our first half. That's why those young people in the workplace might be quicker to pick up new systems and make less mistakes. But Crystallised Intelligence, the accumulation of facts and knowledge, unsurprisingly peaks in our second half. If your workplace is managing the implementation of complex projects, an older person is more likely to navigate to a successful outcome and make less mistakes, because they've been through it all before. So those human resources people need to reconsider the biases in their selection processes!

Matt: The other thing that's spinning through my mind here is that if you are part of an indigenous community, you may not relate to ageism. In cultures where longevity is celebrated, elders are revered for their wisdom. They become the storytellers, the bearers of ancestral knowledge and the architects of a legacy that transcends generations.

Instead of being a disadvantage, age earns the right to take on a role of teaching, sharing knowledge, governance, leadership and community wellbeing. They are invited to oversee ceremony and spiritual practice, which brings them into the centre of the community.

Contrast this with the Western paradigm, where ageing often signals a retreat from active engagement, and an embrace of the stereotype that suggests life's grand pursuits are behind us. It's more common to feel like elders are seen as a burden, often discarded or placed into broken aged care systems. No wonder we dread ageing!

The legacy we leave behind is not merely etched in stone or written on parchment: it's woven into the very fabric of human connection. There's much to learn about growing older from cultures that view ageing as a privilege. Unfortunately, many of us live in societies that don't value ageing, and that impacts our own view, even if we don't want it to. Retirement becomes synonymous with the relentless pursuit of comfort, a retreat into the shadows of our former selves. But I refuse to succumb to such limitations. I say, "Fuck that!"

Susan: You took the words right out of my mouth!

In cultures where longevity is celebrated, elders are revered for their wisdom. They become the storytellers, the bearers of ancestral knowledge and the architects of a legacy that transcends generations.

Awakenings

It was now Susan's turn to share. "What about your story?" I probed. "When did you first start thinking you might be getting old?"

Susan: It was subtle, more of a quiet realisation than a grand event. And I don't think I particularly thought about getting old. It was more a sense that I had entered a new stage of life, and it put me off balance for a while.

I was working with a new client, and in one of my early meetings with their team, I suddenly felt out of place. Instead of being surrounded by older colleagues, I noticed I was one of the older ones. I even asked the human resources person, "Do you intentionally hire so many young managers?" She looked at me with a puzzled face and replied, "No …" As her voice trailed off, it dawned on me: I wasn't surrounded by youth, I was just … older.

For a while, I wondered if my ideas might be outdated. I started to feel invisible and my confidence took a knock. But like you, Matt, all of those self-doubts were based on a fear of other people's perceptions, not on reality.

Matt: You're completely right, Susan. People often seek my advice, and I feel fit – physically, mentally and emotionally. I love supporting the organisations I work with. I took it as a stark reminder of how subtle and powerful external perceptions can be. It took just one comment for those negative thoughts to start looping through my mind, then it took a month of hard work to turn them around. I had to consciously adapt my thinking and focus on being vibrant, happy, influential and wise.

I can see how it could have set me on a path to a midlife crisis, and it was a valuable lesson in maintaining my overall wellbeing. What about you, Susan? What did you do?

Susan: I decided to become a rock drummer!

Matt: That's extreme.

Susan: I'd never picked up a drumstick in my life, but turning 50 felt like the right time to try something new.

Matt: Tell me more about this!

Susan: You should have heard the reactions: "You've taken up the drums? What made you do that at your age?" Others just rolled their eyes. "Are you starting a rock band at 50?" they laughed. *Why not?* I thought. But I kept those thoughts to myself to avoid more criticism.

Some asked if it was a midlife crisis. At the time, I honestly thought drumming was just a spur-of-the-moment decision that seemed like fun. I imagined performing a surprise solo at my 50th birthday party — proof that I still had youth inside me despite the candles on the cake. But when I found myself in a music store buying an electronic drum kit, my middle-aged mind said maybe this was an act of defiance in the face of ageing. When you're in the middle of transitions like this, confusion is normal. You're making decisions that no-one sees coming, not even you.

Maybe there was also some regret over passions left unexpressed; I didn't want to leave anything on the table. Drumming had been a childhood dream, but somewhere along the way I'd settled for air drumming during long car rides.

If I'm honest, I was also a little bored and looking for some excitement in life. My kids needed me less, and instead of projecting loss onto them, I needed to rediscover the beat of my own drum.

Matt: That sounds like quite an awakening.

Susan: It was, but it wasn't all fun and games. In the beginning, it was mostly terror. Learning something new made me feel a bit lost. I did a lot of overthinking, and I had moments of genuine rage. But it's been a few years now and I'm still enjoying it. I've even joined a band!

Matt: Your story about drumming beautifully illustrates a difference I've noticed between how men and women approach midlife transitions. Women often seek new challenges for relevance, while men tend to look back on past accomplishments for validation. Both perspectives have their pitfalls, yet they also possess immense power when combined with self-awareness.

Susan: It's true that a midlife reinvention can present differently between the sexes. Men are often reacting to the feeling of being 'trapped', and the deep desire to escape the burdens of their first half and feel freedom again. Around midlife, men might also grieve what they have lost. The thrill of a career at the top of his game is now just the hard slog of dragging himself out of bed, wondering whether anyone will even notice if he's at work. Female attention and admiration for his good looks and physique may have evolved into a side glance from the dog and disparaging comments from the kids about his 'dad bod'. His bank balance heads towards the red, having been divided a couple of times from relationships gone wrong. A body that comfortably ran miles, now cries out for attention in the form of aches and pains. Or maybe he just isn't where he thought he would be by now.

While a woman can no doubt relate to all of the above, her crisis is often triggered, not by loss, but by a deep call for expansion. As a result of major relationship changes or significant health challenges, often triggered by menopause, she suddenly realises that the thing she wants most is to put more focus back on herself and live a more meaningful life. She spends her nights wondering whether there's still time to quit her job at the accounting desk and take up her dream career. She's already done all her 'missing out' in the first half of life, and now she yearns for more: *Have I explored all that my sexuality/potential/travel has to offer?*

Women often seek new challenges for relevance, while men tend to look back on past accomplishments for validation.

Matt: What you say makes sense when I think of a close female friend. She harboured resentment and anger towards her husband, having sacrificed her career to raise their children, while he built an impressive international career in the sports industry. Her positive transformation began when she started leveraging her considerable skills to develop a unique property portfolio. This transition wasn't just a shift in her mentality; it revitalised her, and helped her overcome stress-related health issues. She also found that it reconnected her with her husband. By focusing on the opportunities available to her, irrespective of her past sacrifices and age, she rediscovered the beautiful, dynamic person she truly is.

Susan: We all just need a spark to ignite us. It can be something minor like the comment about your age in your email address, or it can be something significant. I watched a friend transform her entire life at 55. One year earlier, she was faced with a breast cancer diagnosis, and it shook her to the core. During her process of recovery, she questioned everything. She scrutinised the relationships around her, and realised she was surrounded by people who kept her stuck. As they aged, they had become more negative, cynical and whingy than ever before. So, she found new connections, interests and perspectives on life. "I feel better and am happier than I have ever been," she tells us regularly.

Men are often called to their awakening through career dissatisfaction or changes in the workplace. One of my coaching clients quit his long-held job when he was 58. The final straw was meeting his new boss, a 25-year-old who knew all the answers. He realised his employer saw him as a dinosaur, and he finally acknowledged that he'd been feeling irrelevant for at least a decade. He hated his job and could find no sense of purpose there; it impacted everything in his life. When it all got too much, he took the leap and did what he really wanted to do – he started his own business.

Matt: My own story sheds light on the insecurities many men face in the second half of life, particularly the fear of losing significance and becoming 'less'. Being a professional sportsperson in Australia comes with pretty high expectations about performance, and when you can't maintain it, you really feel like you're losing everything.

As I navigate the landscape of my own second half, I am acutely aware of the finite nature of this adventure. It's a realisation that has become both my compass and my driving force, urging me to defy the societal norms that attempt to confine the latter years of life to a script of decline and repose.

Chapter 4

Changing Demographics

Susan has a way of delivering truth bombs. "Matt, I think people are as afraid of living as they are of death these days." Backing up her conclusion, she continued: "The survey we did in late 2024 told us almost half the people in their second half of life are in survival mode. And men are doing worse than women![2] Why aren't we all thriving? Most people have worked hard for half their life, so shouldn't our second half be the time when we reap the rewards of all that effort?"

Matt: Well, there was a health pandemic in the not-too-distant past, and we're still experiencing the signs of an economic crisis. Maybe that explains why the survey told us the 2 main areas of concern for older people are health and finances, regardless of whether you are male or female.

Susan: Many people are getting stuck in the 'builder' phase of their life. With rising costs of living and delayed parenthood, they often find themselves shouldering significant financial burdens for their children, whether it's saving for a house deposit or paying off university debts. This shift extends financial obligations well into the later years of life, impacting retirement plans and personal freedom.

---

2 - See References 2.

Striving to improve your children's opportunities comes at a cost to your own stress levels and overall wellbeing. I'm certainly not saying we shouldn't make these choices; what I am saying is that we also need to start establishing the conditions to thrive in our second half, or we'll never realise the full potential of this phase of life.

My parents were financially independent from my sister and I in their late 40s. They said, "Goodbye, stand on your own 2 feet and have the resilience to bounce back from the challenges life throws at you." I am so grateful for that, plus they have now had close to 40 years just living their best lives. I acknowledge that things have changed in one generation, but I still feel it's possible for us to make similar choices now.

Happiness researchers have found there's a U-shape when it comes to mapping satisfaction over a lifetime.[3] We start our lives out pretty happy (I mean why wouldn't you: no bills, responsibilities, nothing much to do but eat and play). In the 30 or so years from adolescence to middle age, life satisfaction scores dip around 5-10 percent. As we head into our 50s, happiness begins to take off again, hitting a peak in our 60s.

The problem is, our survey showed that people aren't really happy until their 70s. That's too late! Happiness is poised for its second wind a lot earlier than that, but it won't arise if we delay the natural evolution that our body, mind and spirit craves.

Matt: This makes me think of Wayne Dyer's 2010 spiritual film and book, *The Shift*[4]. He provided a comparison of how our needs deviate during this important midlife transition:

---

3 - See References 3.
4 - See References 4.

Early Life Priorities	Later Life Priorities	Early Life Priorities	Later Life Priorities
Women		**Men**	
1. Family – taking care of everyone	1. Personal growth	1. Wealth	1. Spirituality
2. Independence	2. Self-esteem	2. Sense of adventure	2. Personal peace
3. Career	3. Spirituality	3. Achievement	3. Family
4. Fitting in	4. Happiness	4. Pleasure	4. God's will – sense of purpose
5. Attractiveness	5. Generosity	5. Respect	5. Honesty

Even though it highlights subtle differences between men and women, it's really just the order and timing that's different. Now, more than ever before, it's obvious that first-half priorities for all of us are made up of some combination of:

- *Building the foundations for a career (education, employment)*
- *Finding your tribe (partner, family, friends)*
- *Establishing your financial security (income, investments)*

- *Contributing to the next generation (raise children, lead teams, mentor people)*
- *Enjoying life's pleasures (travel, hobbies, sporting interests)*

While finance and health continued to dominate into the second half for both women and men in our survey, when you read beneath the surface, women were more likely than men to prioritise career achievement in their second half. They also had 'travel to new places' as their top goal, as opposed to 'finance' for men.

Susan: I get why. Women have had a lifetime nurturing connections, raising families, looking after elderly parents, and generally being the Chief Social Coordinator for the family. Midlife may be the first time they can prioritise themselves. Many women return to study, launch a business, or finally go after their long-held dream around this time, just when men are beginning to prioritise family and health. It might be interpreted that they are seeking delayed career achievement, but I suspect it's more about personal growth.

For most women, self-worth is directly linked to relationships and our associations with others: how well you've raised the family, how much you've inspired a team, or whether you have a great group of friends. Being socially connected in community and caring for others generates an internal pride that cannot be underestimated.

It's quite a different experience to that of men, who tend to be more externally focused when it comes to their sense of worth. They are more likely to judge themselves on the success of their mission in the world, their achievements and their financial status.

In the second half, this appears to swap between the sexes. Women start thinking about moving beyond their front gate to explore what they want to do in the external world. In my 40s, I wrote 4 books, went to Spain 3 times to study as a kundalini yoga teacher, went to more conferences than I can remember, and personal growth was a key priority. It was the period of time in my life when I focused most on my growth, confidence, learning and spirituality.

Matt: I definitely identify with what you are saying, Susan. Becoming a granddad at 51 and welcoming 4 grandchildren has given me a new perspective on life. Conversations with my friends have shifted from reminiscing about our wild university days to discussing how we can support and impart wisdom to our grandchildren. Men reach a point when they want to be around their family more. For many, it's about making up for the time they spent working late at the office or travelling away from home.

Susan: Many women talk about watching their husbands or partners getting very involved in their grandchildren's lives, which can only be a good thing. But they also talk about them becoming more reclusive: "He just wants to hang around all the time. All of a sudden, he is the gourmet cook, searching through cooking magazines and trying new things. Where was Mr Chef when I was racing home from work, juggling 2 kids and trying to get dinner on the table?!"

Matt: (chuckling) ... This shift highlights the importance of self-awareness and adapting our roles as we age. We can find a lot of happiness in the second half, by letting this midlife evolution roll forward. Resisting these urges can make the second half stressful.

While Wayne Dyer's comparison still feels very true to me, our 2024 survey suggests many people are delaying these later life priorities. The changing demographics of our times might be one reason. According to UN projections, in the year 2100 there will be more 80-year-olds and 100-year-olds than in the whole of human history. Since the 1900s, we have added over 3 decades of life expectancy, so midlife and beyond now take up a large portion of our lives. The obvious milestones of ageing, like kids leaving home, parents passing away and retirement, seem to happen later in life for many people. Reaching midlife (remember, that's generally in your 40s), often gets missed in all the noise of these drawn-out, first-half activities.

I can relate. I was establishing my footy career, building my finances, having a family, and using my physical skills to achieve peak performance in my sport. I couldn't expect to keep performing at the highest level in my sport beyond a certain age, so that meant I had to build a whole new career as a team coach when I was in my 30s, then as a mindset and leadership coach in my 50s.

I don't want to stop working just because I'm in my second half — that's definitely not our message to people reading this book. My work fulfils the goals I have for my second half: to be inspired, to inspire others, and to maintain my own physical, mental, emotional and spiritual health. I just refuse to delay my happiness anymore.

Susan: I think the significant focus on finances can hinder many people from taking the steps we're talking about in this book. We're not finance experts, and there are plenty of resources for people to turn to for guidance on setting themselves up for a financially abundant second half, but I do have some observations about mindsets that could be at play.

Many people haven't determined how much they really need for a comfortable second half, especially how much they need before they can stop work. In the absence of facts, we create uncertainty in our minds. Uncertainty disrupts our normal, rational cognitive processes and tips us into a hypervigilant state, to ensure our survival. This may explain why many of our survey respondents indicated they were in survival mode. We see them continuing in builder phase, because they feel they don't have 'enough'. But I wonder if that's true for all of them?

Matt: I think you're onto something there, Susan. Let me tell you about a conversation I had with a female client. I remember saying, "I'm not sure how I can help you, unless you reframe your perspective on life and gain genuine clarity about what you truly want."

She owned a thriving design and marketing business, with a global workforce of over 100 people. Her business was booming in Australia and overseas, and the profits were impressive. Her husband ran a successful construction business, and they lived in an affluent suburb of Sydney. They had 2 delightful children in primary school. When I visited for our mindset and mindfulness sessions, the fun they brought made me want to hang out with them.

"I've shared this with you before, Matt. I want the company to generate over $15 million in profit every year for the next decade, so I can slowly withdraw from day-to-day operations," she said.

"Why do you want to do that?" I asked.

"So, I can sit back, enjoy life, spend time with my kids, and go on family adventures. We've covered this before," she replied sharply.

"But why do you want to do those things?" I pressed.

"I told you, so I can enjoy life and be happy."

"Then why have you brought me here? I can't help with your business; I'd probably run it into the ground in a week," I joked.

"Matt, I know you're pissing me off again. I have you here because I'm struggling to stay on top of things. I feel stressed, like I'm not good enough, and that makes me feel hollow."

"I love working with you, because you cut to the chase. So, this time, sit back, do your breathing and answer this question: Can you be happy and enjoy life now, or do you need to wait until all your goals are achieved before you can be happy?"

"That's easier said than done."

"Answer the question."

"Yes, I can."

"If you're sure about that, we can use all the mindset and lifestyle tools I'm sharing with you to make this a reality. It doesn't mean all the challenges of running a successful business will disappear. It means you'll reframe them as achievements and opportunities for personal growth. It also means you won't wait until the business reaches a certain level before you feel pride and self-worth. You'll take time daily to love your life, family and yourself. You'll empower others, so you can enjoy incredible adventures with those you love now, not in a decade. Waiting only leads to regret."

That conversation was pivotal for my client. Although she wasn't very animated at the time and was a bit cranky with me, things started to change. Our sessions began to focus more on what she was proud of, how much time she scheduled for her kids and husband, when the next exciting adventure was planned, and the realisation that her business was something she'd created, not who she was.

Chapter 5

Mindset Matters

We were beginning to get to the crux of the matter, and I continued with my point: "I've worked with many affluent people, and also those facing financial challenges. We are conditioned to associate abundance with our bank accounts, but some of my wealthiest clients have been the most miserable. Financial security is wonderful, and it provides opportunities, but if you don't consciously choose to be happy and enjoy life, you're left with merely surviving."

Susan: Choosing your mindset is such a crucial step. You decide how you want to 'be' in life, and it's the foundation for everything that comes next.

Matt: Sometimes we think things are happening because of our age, but they really happen because of our mindset. For example, I find myself single at this stage, contemplating whether my soulmate will emerge into my life. Simultaneously, a close friend, married for over 30 years, ponders the worth of continuing a lifelong partnership that has weathered the storms of time, but perhaps moved in different directions. The commonality is not in the age bracket, but in the tendency to make our circumstances about our vintage, rather than the actual situation we aim to resolve. The thing that does matter in the second half is that you don't keep putting things off.

Susan: I'm sorry, but this brings me back to funerals. No-one spends their final hours wishing they'd worked harder, or accumulated just a bit more wealth, or bought more stuff to store in their garage.

Matt: What do you think the regrets would be on your death bed?

Susan: Well, I'm definitely not qualified in this area, but I know someone who is. Bronnie Ware wrote the book, *The Top 5 Regrets of the Dying*, based on her years supporting people in palliative care. You probably won't be surprised to know that not a single regret was about working harder. In fact, one of the top regrets was actually working too hard. Bronnie said that every single man she spoke to had this regret, and wished he'd spent more time in his important relationships.

Matt: I can see why that would happen for men. Sometimes our provider instinct stops us from seeing what's really important. I'm curious, what were the other regrets?

Susan: *I wish I lived a life true to myself and not the life others expected of me.*

Matt: Yes! I think that's why it's so important to have the conversations we're having, and to bust the myths of what we 'should' be doing, or what society tells us are the priorities in the second half.

Susan: The next one is: *I wish I had the courage to express my feelings.*

Matt: That one hits me hard. It's such a difficult one for men.

Susan: It might surprise you to hear it, but it's difficult for women too. We've grown up thinking we need to be 'pretty and nice' and watched women get labelled 'crazy' for expressing emotions.

one of the top regrets of the dying was actually working too hard.

Matt: Men's conditioning is also not to express emotion. We're going to talk about a lot more, and I'm so glad we have dedicated a whole chapter to emotions. Bronnie's book just confirms how important it is. What else?

Susan: *I wish I'd stayed in touch with my friends.*

Matt: Family and relationships came out as a high priority for both men and women in our survey too. Everyone seems to have the insight that it's important, but I wonder how many people put it into practice? I know I let busyness stand in the way sometimes.

Susan: Me too. But I agree it's so important, and we'll talk about it more in the spirituality chapter.

Okay, last one sums it all up really: *I wish I had let myself be happier.*

Matt: So simple. But I am reminded by our survey that only around half of us are thriving. We need that figure to be 100%, and with a bit of awareness, intent and effort, I know we can all achieve it. I feel like this is my deepest motivation for writing this book. Only you have the power to 'let yourself' be happier.

Vibrancy, fun, learning, intimacy and purpose are not reserved for the young. They are capacities accessible to us every day, and this book is a guide to unlocking and growing these aspects of life.

But I realise that's easier said than done, particularly for women in this phase of life. That's why I'm grateful to be talking to you Susan. It's important to have a female voice in this discussion. The experience is different for women. I can't pretend to even try to understand what it must be like facing a major life transition and menopause at the same time.

you are capable of far more than you might currently believe.

Susan: It's not easy, that's for sure. It's definitely not the same as the male experience, and I am glad we are shedding light on this topic of conversation.

Matt: I can't wait to learn and understand the many differences, but regardless of our differences, we will all feel physical, mental, emotional and spiritual changes during midlife. How we navigate those will dictate how we experience the rest of our lives. Some of the solutions will be the same for all of us, and some will be different. We don't assume to predict your responses or assert that our suggestions offer a one-size-fits-all solution. Our goal is to elevate your self-awareness, and help you cultivate a belief that you are capable of far more than you might currently believe. No matter what your sex or identity, entering the second half is a time when you will naturally put all your beliefs under the microscope. You may recognise lack or inadequacy in areas of your life, and the past might come up and hit you in the face again. Your empty nest might feel lonely, and you might believe it's not possible to find new adventures this late in life. Maybe you'll question why you made the choices you made. Regret, remorse, resentment and guilt may arise.

Susan: Instead of letting these feelings define your second half, treat them as signals that guide you towards a new level of joy. Let go of whatever holds you back, and reconnect to your playfulness and your superpowers. You're at a crossroad, and here are your choices:

1. *You can leap into the second half of the game with a renewed commitment to your health, relationships, wellbeing and purpose;*

or

2. *You can give up and retire to the bench.*

Matt: Yes! This book is about getting on the front foot, and running into the game with strength, vision and an attitude of opportunity. No matter what age you are, as you read these words, the time to consider ageing is now. The person you will be when you're 80 depends largely on the choices you make in your 40s, 50s and beyond. It truly is the best time of your life, if you choose to see it that way.

We're presenting an invitation to challenge the status quo, to question the restrictive norms that cast a shadow over the latter years of life. The anecdotes and insights within these pages are testament to the fact that, just like a fine wine, life can get better with age. The second half of life is not a spectator sport; it's a grand stage on which we have the power to redefine what it means to live vibrantly and leave a legacy that resonates far beyond our years.

But Susan, you know what I want to dive into next?

*The second half of life is
not a spectator sport.*

Susan: Let me guess. You want to know about secret women's business, don't you?

Matt: Guessed it in one. Let's do it!

Section 2
Secret Women's Business

Chapter 6

The Female Narrative

I was looking forward to sitting down and listening to Susan's perspective on this one, even if it wasn't aimed at me or men in general. Understanding the perspective of women is key to deepening our relationships and therefore our experience of the second half.

Susan: This chapter speaks primarily to women, but men, please don't stop reading. We're going to explore the many obstacles that women face to thriving in our second half. Yes, that means we will definitely talk about menopause and other things women often keep to themselves, but Matt, you're welcome to eavesdrop because I've found that a guy who tries to understand what women go through (and shares what he's going through) is the sort of guy most women want in their life.

Matt: I promise to listen fully, Susan. I have to confess that my understanding of women moving into the second half of life is pretty limited, much like most of my mates. As a bloke with a lot of female friends, and a dad of 4 daughters (a fact I'll probably mention 100 times), I'm not coming from a place of finding women perplexing, but rather from a position of having little awareness of the unique challenges they face. I've never had the opportunity to listen in on secret women's business. Or maybe I wasn't ready to do that until now. So, I promise to stay quiet and listen ... well, I'll try to stay quiet!

Susan: Let me take you back nearly 25 years to an event that is burnt into my memory. I looked up in awe at her small figure, perched on a simple chair in the centre of the stage. Her blonde hair cascaded gently to her shoulders. She had a radiance that beamed towards the audience like a rising sun. My 30-year-old self dreamt to be her.

Louise Hay was stunning, wise and all-knowing. She'd sold more than 50 million copies of her first book, *You Can Heal Your Life*, and authored many more. She founded Hay House, the most popular self-help publishing house in the world, launching the career of many other famous writers who were changing people's lives. During this visit to Australia, I'm guessing she was in her late 70s, and she was at the top of her game.

She was quite a contrast to my grandma, who was wearing slippers and rocking in her recliner at that age. My mind wandered, imagining the lifetime of success she must have enjoyed: *What had she already achieved at 30? Am I too late? Maybe I haven't achieved enough to be on the trajectory to that kind of greatness?*

Then Louise's voice snapped me out of my dreamlike state: "My first published book was released in 1984."

My eyes darted around as the calculations went through my head. Wait, what?! The realisation nearly knocked me off my cheap plastic seat. She wrote a book and was discovered by the world when she was 58 years old. The majority of her success happened after that age, in her 60s, 70s and even 80s.

I never looked at ageing the same way again. A decade or so after watching her on stage, when Louise was in her 80s, I was ecstatic to hear that she was rockin' out with a much, much younger boyfriend. What a queen! The late Louise Hay's legacy lives on, an inspiration to all women entering their second half.

I'm grateful for my experience that day. After all, if you can't see it, you can't be it.

However, it also highlighted that, despite being a feminist and a life-loving go-getter, I had a very poor narrative around women's worth as we age.

What are the first thoughts that come to mind when you hear the term 'middle-aged woman'? Do you envision positive images of a confident, energised, sexy woman thriving in the prime years of her life, or an exhausted and cranky one, with bumps in all the wrong places? Don't beat yourself up too much for negative associations. This chapter promises to offer you food for thought and myth-busting motivation to embrace a narrative that says your second half can be fabulous. Until you face your own outdated narrative, none of the useful tips we share in this book will get traction.

We've got to call out the unhelpful stuff, those stereotypes and assumptions about middle-aged women that no longer apply to those of us passing through midlife right now. I can't identify with ads on TV for retirement villages or funeral insurance, where the grey-haired lady with the good-natured smile is playing bowls with similarly docile friends, or tending the garden with her husband. They belong to my parents' era, people beyond their 70s.

There seems to be little genuine effort to genuinely portray those of us in our 40s, 50s and 60s, who are passing through midlife and beginning our second-half adventures in a world that's changing at warp speed. I can't point to any advertising that reflects the real life I'm inhabiting, or the reality for most of my friends. That's not to say some of us don't have great role models in our personal life, and I can point to quite a few public women too: actors like Helen Mirren, who is undeniably sassy; Demi Moore, who is having a moment again at 62 years of age; and Naomi Watts, who is advocating to demystify menopause. The numbers of impressive older women in public life are growing, but they are still the exceptions.

It's hard to change your narrative when your neurons have absorbed the sting from watching countless ageing female TV personalities being retired, stories of wives being upgraded to a younger model, or comments that a woman is "too old to be wearing that colourful outfit". There are subtle messages everywhere, spinning the story that women should be invisible as they age. The ageing male newsreader is a 'silver fox' but his co-presenter is an 'old boiler'. Gosh, I'm getting fired up just thinking about it!

But this is not a blame game. First impressions really do stick, and your brain wires up your worldview from that foundation. The first person most of us would have been exposed to in their second half was a grandparent. Forty years ago, grandparents were probably retired, maybe cruising off on their one big international trip, then settling in to tend their garden, before passing away in their 70s. Sounds harsh, but the average lifespan in Australia in the 1960s was 71 years of age.

Sure, the pre-retirement crowd was still working, but all I saw were old white men in the boss positions around town. I can't remember any women filling those roles. Maybe there was a librarian or a school teacher. Yes, I know it sounds like I'm regurgitating stereotypes, but back then they were pretty accurate. Only a generation ago, most workplaces required women to step aside when they got married, and resign when having kids. A woman's success was measured by her ability to acquire and keep a husband, maintain a harmonious home, and raise good children. Her prospects after the kids left the nest? For many women, not much.

If you were exposed to this image of society in every direction you looked, how could your brain have wired up a positive narrative about adventure, success, freedom and achievement in your second half? And given that our lifespans are likely to be longer, if you're not planning to be engaged, productive and joyful, what are you going to do with the decades that lie before you?

if you can't see it, you can't be it.

Chapter 7

A New Narrative

I was fascinated. So many questions were circling in my mind as Susan shared her thoughts.

Susan: Ageing is changing, and it's about time society caught up. We need a new narrative around women in their second half. It's got to be one that sets us free to bring forth our wisdom, energy and spirit, without feeling blocked, ignored or dismissed. But if part of you is still buying into the old narrative, you'll struggle to fulfil your second half potential.

We need to bust the myths and stereotypes that are deeply entrenched in our culture. Some of them will make you smile because, frankly, they are laughable. Others might make you feel sad that anyone in the world would dare think this way. But it doesn't matter, because we're going to flip them on their heads. If you're prepared to think differently and create your own new narrative, you'll be ready to fully embrace the tips around wellness and longevity that we'll share with you in coming chapters.

Matt: Susan, sorry to jump in, but I'm curious – what's your new narrative? Are you willing to share that now?

Susan: I think each woman needs to define it in her own words, but I'm happy to share what I believe about the potential of a woman in her second half.

A New Narrative

She is fiercely independent. She is confident and creative. She exudes a combination of inner and outer beauty. She boldly breaks with protocol and walks her own talk. She doesn't care what you think of her, but she cares deeply about the world. She is sexually awakened, not depleted. She is sovereign, not under the control of anyone but herself. She's acquired wisdom through her experience, and it's a form of wisdom that can change the world for the better.

I believe women can be at their best and most powerful in the second half of their life. Oh, and let's not forget ... grey is the new black. When we fully embody all that's positive about our phase of life, we look hot!

Matt: I've got to say I totally agree. I find that women are far more judgemental of other women than men are. Personally, I wouldn't give 2 shits what dress, shoes or make-up my partner has on, but hooley dooley, the obsession about appearance between women is mind-blowing: "Nice mascara," "That highlighter she has on is terrible," "Where did you buy those earrings?" "What do you think of her hairdo?". A typical male response is, "What would you like to drink?"

Susan: Ha! You're pretty right there, Matt. You'd think that would only apply to younger women, but we commonly reinforce that ageist attitude with each other:

- *She looks good ... for her age.*
- *She's dressed like a 30-year-old!*
- *She'd look much better if she covered those greys.*

Actually, you've highlighted the first of 4 myths we need to bust.

Myth 1: Youth Is Synonymous with High Worth and Value

We are constantly exposed to signals that our value declines as we age. Local jargon and slang contain so much of our cultural messaging, and terms like the following are a dead giveaway for how older women are viewed: biddy, old hag, crone, witch, old bag, blue rinse set.

I'm sure people from different countries and cultures could list others. Interestingly, I can't quickly name many for men.

Matt: Grumpy old bastard, old codger, has-been, fogey, pale and stale ...

Susan: Okay, fair enough. But let's face it, women are more likely to encounter ageist attitudes. As you said, we even do it to each other. The result of buying into this myth is that women are spending billions on beauty products to 'help us to stay young'. At the time of publication, the global beauty industry was worth $511 billion dollars, and a significant contribution is made by women over 50 undertaking cosmetic procedures aimed at retaining their youth.

Now, before you feel any sense of judgement, please know that's not my intention. Beauty is serious business for women, and I'm buying the face creams too. That's because I want to take the very best care of this body by moisturising my cells and protecting them from the sun. What concerns me is that the rise in the number of anti-ageing products and services highlights how vulnerable we are to the narrative that says 'youth is better'. And it's not just affecting our age group. More and more girls are guarding against ageing in later life (or so they believe) by commencing botox and anti-ageing procedures in their teens. We need to change this narrative, not only for ourselves, but also for future generations.

Youth has its time and place, but it is not better than age. Diarist and author, Anais Nin, said: *"Life is a process of becoming, a combination of states we have to go through. Where people fail is that they wish to elect a state and remain in it. This is a kind of death."* When we try to retain aspects of youth that will naturally fade, we're missing the chance to embrace aspects of ageing that are just as valuable: wisdom, serenity, confidence, insight and intuition, to name just a few.

"Life is a process of becoming, a combination of states we have to go through. Where people fail is that they wish to elect a state and remain in it. This is a kind of death."

Anais Nin, diarist and author

Chapter 8

Creative Woman, Nurturing Woman, Wise Woman

We found ourselves talking about Jung again, then ancient philosophies. I must admit I love all that stuff. It really makes you think.

Susan: Just as Jung said, we need to understand and appreciate our cyclical nature. A woman's basic nature is very different to that of a man. Men are like the sun. Women are like the moon. In many spiritual and ancient traditions, the sun is seen as a masculine concept, and the moon is feminine. Why? Well, one thing is guaranteed: the sun rises every morning and sets every evening. It is a consistent and stable force that can be relied on to provide the structure of the day. We couldn't exist without it, and when you're with a healthy form of masculine, you'll notice the same. Men will provide structure, security, safety, stability, direction and leadership. Nothing says it better than those mushy Instagram posts from women referring to masculine partners as 'my rock', 'my grounding force'.

As the moon goes through its monthly cycles, it effects all sorts of change and chaos. Women are familiar with cycles in their lives. Our monthly cycle is the obvious one, but we experience other hormonal cycles, physical cycles and emotional cycles. Ancient teachings tell us that a woman moves to a new moon centre every 2.5 days, and this readjustment changes her mood and outlook. No wonder so many men are confused by us. They have just one moon centre to our 11!

Matt: If my view represents most men, we see women as far less complicated than all that. In fact, any male who says they understand this is full of shit. I've certainly had my fair share of insights, but not for one second would I pretend to understand. My simple view of women would be Mother Earth, providing uncompromising care and forever giving, but if you want to fuck with her, there's a cyclone or earthquake coming your way. Just like Mother Earth, men take this care for granted, and ignore the impacts of their actions on the environment.

Susan: Well, Matt, there are at least 3 distinct phases in a woman's life, all equally important and impactful. It's only when you stand at middle age and look back that these stages become clear, even to us.

The **Creative Woman** represents the early phase of life, as the girl becomes a woman. It's a time of independence, self-discovery and exploration. Life is meant to be tasted and, in this phase, she is liberated and free. Youth, purity and fertility are all at play. It's a woman's springtime, the phase before she becomes a mother or takes on nurturing responsibilities. It's difficult to put an age on this phase, because it can shift as society evolves. For example, our mothers and grandmothers may have started their families in their early 20s, whereas now it's not uncommon to delay that phase shift into, and beyond, a woman's 30s.

It's important for a young woman to experience the **Creative Woman** phase, and cutting it short can have consequences. Personally, I had 2 shots at this phase. I got married when I was 22 and tried to enter the next phase of nurturing responsibilities way too early (for me). While this works for many people, I had not done enough exploration, or experienced enough freedom, and I simply didn't know myself. This resulted in a divorce at 28. It was the time between then and having my first child at 34 that I really experienced the gifts this phase has to offer. I played, studied different things, enjoyed many relationships, tried out different jobs, lived in different places, travelled, and generally enjoyed the pleasures of life. I learnt about my impact as an individual before I began a life in service to others.

When a woman exits the **Creative Woman** phase, she enters the **Nurturing Woman** phase. This is when her nurturing capabilities come to the fore. She finds meaning in her devotion and service to others. It's important to mention that you don't have to have children to relate to this stage. If you're a woman who has chosen a different path, you will equally enter this phase and meet your nurturing needs in other ways. You might have a purposeful career or look after a team of people. You might be a passionate cat or dog mum, an involved aunt, or care for elderly parents. You may be saving the planet, solving community problems or working hard for a cause. It can look different for all of us, but I experienced this phase between about 32 and 45 years of age. During this time, I had 2 children but I also discovered my purpose. I finally understood how I wanted to be in service to the world, and I birthed a business, found joy in mentoring people, and wrote 3 books because of a strong desire to share my messages with the world.

The third phase, which I hit around age 45, is the **Wise Woman** stage. Believe me, it didn't look that wise when the calendar hit 45; but looking back, I can see this is when the transformation began. The **Wise Woman** is in the second half of her life and is the embodiment of women's wisdom, power and intuition. She sits fully in her power and has integrated all her years of knowledge and experience into wisdom. She is now in a position to share it with the world.

By the time a woman has reached the second half of her life, she is a confident expert of her craft. Her intuitive and creative ideas are married with great experience in the practicalities of the world. She is free from both ego and insecurity, and grounded in her emotions. Her heart and sexuality are awakened. She's not bothered by what other people think.

- ✓ The insecure girl has become a confident woman.
- ✓ The girl seeking everything outside of herself has become deeply fulfilled.
- ✓ The body hater is now joyfully embodied.
- ✓ The people pleaser has evolved into a queen, whose approval others try to gain.
- ✓ The victim is now powerful.
- ✓ The shy has turned fierce.
- ✓ The 'pretty and nice' has become 'beautiful and bold'.

Standing at half-time in your life, you've finally arrived. But why doesn't it feel like that? Because no transition is easy. Our minds lag behind our bodies, and we've still got a few myths to bust so we can catch up to ourselves.

Chapter 9

Stop. Rest. Re-energise. Celebrate.

I was hanging on the edge of my seat waiting to hear more about these myths Susan was exploring.

Susan: It's time to explore the second of the 4 myths we need to bust.

Myth 2: Your Best Years Are Behind You

In a world of 'quick have it now', child superstars and 20-year-old online millionaires, it's easy to fall into the trap of believing that the highlights of your life reel are behind you, once you hit the second half. But what if you stopped to consider the possibility that your life could be its most abundant, fulfilling and enriching in the second half?

Abundance in your second half sounds great, right? But if you're anything like me, it probably sounds a bit exhausting too. Half of you wants to conquer the world, and half of you could sleep for 5 years.

"I'm bone tired," I remember remarking to a childhood friend, as we sat on the shore looking out to the ocean. "It's weird … different from when you feel plain tired. My bones actually feel exhausted, like I can't carry them around anymore." I went on to explain that I should feel relaxed. I had just come off a holiday that went for a couple of months, and I was deliberately monitoring my workload for the last few years, to make sure I stayed in balance. Then it hit me! I wasn't tired from the last few years; I was exhausted from the last 50.

We live in a world that's becoming increasingly busy with every passing day. While the intention of the Creative Woman phase was to frolic in a field of possibilities, chances are you were getting the degree, travelling the world, buying the house and climbing the career ladder. By the time you enter the Nurturing Woman phase, you're depleted before you even start some of the busiest and sleep-deprived days of your life. Nothing quite prepares you for the exhaustion of being a mother, or a leader. Whether you're up feeding your baby or pacing the floor worrying about your team, you'll experience long days, sleepless nights, way too much 'doing' with zero focus on yourself. For most women, by the time they reach the magic years when the Wise Woman can truly be unleashed, they are too freaking exhausted from overdoing the earlier stages. Not to mention doubling down with the exhaustion that can hit with menopause.

Women's lives have changed so much, even in one generation. We're taking on increased responsibilities, juggling more roles and facing a faster pace of living. It all contributes to feeling overloaded, overwhelmed and 'over it'. Yet if you're anything like me, you hardly took a breath between any of it, and never came up for air. Women who are hitting midlife now grew up in the era of 'women can do anything', so anything and everything is what we did! As more jobs landed in our laps, we didn't think to question what we should stop doing. We kept adding to the already full pile.

The world's expectations felt daunting, but they weren't as huge as the expectations we put on ourselves. Back in our mother's and grandmother's generation, a woman tended to judge herself on one thing: Is my house clean and running like clockwork? Nowadays, we judge ourselves on a whole raft of things:

- *Do I live in a great place?*
- *Do I have a fulfilling job?*
- *Am I climbing the career ladder?*
- *Is he a loving partner?*
- *Is this a great sex life?*
- *Are my children perfect?*
- *Are my abs flat?*
- *Are these wrinkles under control?*
- *Is my health thriving?*
- *Do I have holidays and adventures a-plenty?*

You get the picture.

When you hit your fourth and fifth decades, you may be seriously burnt out. That's why it can feel like the best years are behind you. But this is not an ending, it's half-time in the game of life. Before you even think about running back on the field:

Stop / Rest / Re-Energise / Celebrate
You don't need to approach your second half like you did your first. It's not linear, and it's not a race or an uphill climb. You don't need to strive and train – you are prepared for this. Use your accumulated wisdom, lose your fears, set your sights on

fresh and fulfilling goals, and work in harmony with your energy.

The best is yet to come!

Matt: That's made me think about a friend who started a conversation with me, explaining the distance in his relationship. "Mate, she has gone to the next level, and to be honest, I'm not sure how to keep up with her. I have zero idea what direction she is going in, and my ability to have conversations with her is so limited."

I replied, "Tony, you know you're talking to me, right? So, there is a fair bit of evidence I don't get this right either. But if you'd like to learn from my mistakes, I'd suggest showing genuine curiosity. Ask questions about where your wife's priorities are, rather than asking what's wrong."

I'm not sure why so many of my mates come to me for advice, given my track record with relationships. The point is not to focus on what's wrong with this new pursuit of more in life, but to ask the right questions about what is driving this new ambition and how you can support it. This doesn't mean you'll fully understand where the change comes from, but it will provide insight into why it's happening and how you can join in. Equally, if it's outside your area of interest, you don't have to get on board, but you do need to be authentic about your reasons.

Use your accumulated wisdom, lose your fears, set your sights on fresh and fulfilling goals, and work in harmony with your energy.

Chapter 10

The Menopause Mystery

The third myth – this is the one I was waiting for. Could Susan help us men get our heads around this mystery?

Susan: I like to call this myth 'Menopause ruins your sex life/sleep life/whole freaking life!'

Myth 3: Menopause Ruins Your Life

Actually, there's a bit of reality in this one and I don't want to make light of a very serious subject for many women. Fluctuating hormones can wreak havoc on your system, making all those visions of a powerful, energised and joyful midlife challenging. Declining oestrogen and progesterone levels can affect sleep, mood, weight, sex drive, energy levels and leave you in a hot, sweaty mess. I have heard the number 70 often used to highlight the broad range of menopause symptoms that women can experience across their physical, mental and emotional health. How many could you name Matt?

Matt: I'm embarrassed to say, probably only a handful.

Susan: You're not alone. The fact is most of us women are not truly informed on the full scope of menopause symptoms. This astounds me because every single female on the planet goes through it. Symptoms may show up with different levels of severity for each of us, but no woman is exempt from menopause. Personally, I had no idea that my frozen shoulder, sudden bursts of anxiety, recurrent UTI's, mood swings and sleepless nights had anything to do with menopause. Like many women, I sought treatment for each condition separately, unaware they were connected. My doctors never made the link for me either. I have friends who have dealt with extreme symptoms like major depressive episodes, debilitating joint pain, prolonged periods of being awake all night, and constant migraines. It's pretty difficult to embrace your Queen-dom when dealing with that every day! Menopause symptoms can start a decade before your last period in the phase called perimenopause, so this is far from a quick process. For the purpose of educating us all, I have listed some of the more common symptoms in Appendix 1. I'm far from being an expert in menopause but I recommend reading several great books which I have also referenced in the Appendix. Being informed and educated really is the key. We'll get to specific tips for what helped me optimise my physical, mental, emotional and spiritual health in future chapters. But right now, it's useful to reflect on our narrative about menopause.

"Your blood test results indicate you're in menopause," the doctor said, peering over her glasses. Ah, I was wondering why I felt like pausing all the men in my life. But I did feel different – just 'off', nauseous at times, tired, restless and as for the brain fog!

Sweating all over the boardroom at the most inopportune time should have been the giveaway, but yet, the diagnosis didn't sit comfortably with me. "What? I'm too young. This can't be!"

"I'm in menopause!" I exclaimed to my friends, with a slight tinge of shame.

"Oh no, my period is still regular and full," one chimed in, not wanting to be tainted by this dis-ease.

Another woman shared her fears when told her heart palpitations could be linked to menopause: "I don't want to be a dried-up cow being put to the outer paddock." She'd decided not to take the path of having children many years ago, but fertility still represented the prize to her.

Here's what you'll know for sure about menopause from discussions with your mother or girlfriends. First ... nothing! Let's face it, most of us have no idea what we're getting into, because it has never been a topic of conversation. We roll into this phase completely blind. Second, if you do hear something, it's all the negatives. I haven't been in too many conversations with a woman who talks about how uplifting menopause has been for her. In addition, most of the narrative around menopause treatments is negative, fear-based and frankly outdated, leaving many women disempowered and feeling helpless in finding solutions. You don't have to suffer in silence or believe it's all you deserve. It doesn't have to ruin your life. There are better days ahead. Do your own research, advocate for yourself, ask lots of questions, find the treatment and support you need, and educate yourself and the people you share your life with. My kids were met with an annoying education opportunity every time they didn't get what they wanted and put it down to "Mum you are tired and angry all the time."

Aside from the stress of trying to live life while riding a hormonal rollercoaster, menopause comes with complex emotions for women. The end of your period, that familiar friend who turned up every month, means a couple of things: you've reached a new stage, and you're going to save a ton of money by no longer buying sanitary products. As much as you may have whinged about the inconvenience, pain and unfairness of your period for 4 decades, you can't help feeling you've lost something really precious – a certain youthfulness, a feeling of fertility and growth. But at the same time, there's an excitement in moving to another phase. I felt a new sense of courage and freedom, a willingness to show my vulnerability, and confidence to bring forth my creativity and wisdom.

Research shows it's not only the hormonal shift that happens during menopause, but a woman's whole brain and nervous system is rewired during this time.[5] You may have experienced the downside – foggy head, difficulty focusing and often some anxiety – but there's a positive side too. There is more activity in the temporal lobes of your brain, resulting in increased intuitive awareness. The Wise Woman benefits from the fuel being pumped to her brain and nervous system during menopause. If you look at this time with conscious awareness, you can work with these changes, not against them.

It's an emotional time but what if you saw some of the strong feelings that arise unexpectedly during menopause as emotions coming up for attention? You may have suppressed them for years, even decades, but emotional debris needs to be healed before you can fully step into your Wise Woman.

---

5 - See References 5.

"I'm so angry. I need a stiff drink" could be turned into, "I'm having these sharp feelings of anger. What's beneath them? What do I need to process and heal? How can I transmute them?"

When I was in the midst of the annoying hot flushes, I would imagine they were surges bringing all that power distributed throughout my body into the one central atomic place. I still didn't enjoy them but the higher reason I created seemed to help.

"I feel so heavy and tired" could be telling you, "I deserve to catch up on the rest that's owed to me from the last 4 decades. I'm going to stop powering through and start listening to my body."

Perhaps menopause can teach us containment. As women, we often leak our energy all over the place, trying to be everything to everyone. A 'yes' to something is always a 'no' to something else, and chances are the 'no' was to your own creativity and self-care. Now is the right time to prioritise and make good choices around where you will and will not use your energy.

Yes, menopause can be super tough. No change comes without disruption, discomfort and sometimes disillusionment. Will you plummet into an emotional and depressed mess? It's not a given, and even if you do, it's certainly not permanent. Raging hormones hit you at the same time as your inner self presents you with deep questions about life in the second half. It can feel confusing and completely unstable.

But just like healthy thoughts on ageing can increase your longevity, your menopause narrative can impact your experience. What parts of your menopause narrative aren't helping you? How can you turn it into something useful going forward?

Matt: Menopause is particularly challenging for men to understand, because it's not a topic that's often shared openly. My strong suggestion to women in relationships is to take the time to explain what's going on, knowing that you're sharing an insight, rather than expecting your partner to fully understand. The reality is, you have to experience something to truly get it; but gents, elevating your awareness can have multiple positive impacts for yourself and those you love.

Now is the right time to prioritise and make good choices around where you will and will not use your energy.

Susan: I agree, Matt, we shouldn't be hiding this from men as if it's secret women's business. But I'm going to go one step further in advice to men - try to educate yourself too. There are many books and websites available. In the great relationships I know, men are doing their independent research so they can bring a level of understanding and empathy to the table. Together we can get on the front foot and start talking about menopause before it's upon us. Why should it be different to having future conversations with your partner about retirement? Exploring what may and may not happen, and how you will handle the phase together, is critical before you are smack bang in the middle of it.

For women, it can feel like a crisis, but it doesn't have to be. The good news is that our happiness follows a U-shape. We get happier in the later phase of our lives. These emotions could simply be part of the transit. Embrace the messy. Don't worry if you feel like you're falling to pieces. Some days I felt like I was dying. Other days I felt like I was going crazy. This was not comfortable for a woman who was used to being level-headed and in control. But unravelling is part of letting go, and letting go is essential when preparing for the best phase of your life!

But also remember, you don't have to be a martyr struggling through using 'mind control' as your only medicine. There are an increasing number of resources available to treat, educate and support women through menopause. Speak to a trusted health adviser, and get the dialogue going between your friends too. We all have a unique set of experiences, but being in this together is incredibly empowering.

Chapter 11

Elevate to the Top of the Pile

We were up to the fourth and final myth, and I could see Susan was particularly passionate about this one.

Susan: Myth 4 is one I see in so many women. It's the mistaken belief that it's selfish to put yourself first.

Myth 4: It's Selfish to Put Yourself First

Half-time doesn't equate to a number, but rather a feeling. There's a calling or a yearning to embrace something different. It can be triggered by your circumstances, and is often prompted by having more space in your life. As children leave home or gain their independence, your daily time is no longer spent asking questions like, "Have you got your phone?" Instead, you have time to ask yourself: "What will I do now?"

Chances are thinking about yourself will feel uncomfortable and daunting. You're out of practice, but it feels exciting at the same time. If there's one piece of advice I'd give to women entering midlife, it would be this: It's time to elevate yourself to the top of the pile.

I'll bet you shook in your boots just reading that. We've been conditioned for years to take the burnt chop, ensure everyone else is comfortable before settling down, give up an opportunity so someone else can enjoy it, or take the raw end of the deal. Most of the time we've been happy with that, but we need to change as we move through the second half. No longer are you putting on the oxygen mask, just so you can save someone else. It's now about saving your own goddamn life.

As primary caregivers, we can easily fall into the trap of extending the nurturing phase of our lives. Many of our survey respondents admitted they were still in the 'builder' phase of life, even into their 60s and 70s. They talked about chasing financial security, not necessarily for their own retirement, but to set their kids up in life. When you have spent the majority of your life doing things for others rather than yourself, that's not an easy mental and emotional structure to dismantle.

There can be genuine barriers to completely shedding the Nurturing Woman phase; some of you may be caring for elderly parents and some of you might not yet be empty nesters. But it's important to allow space for the Wise Woman phase of your life to unfold. Don't pull away from the call to be powerful and fierce, joyful and bold.

In fact, that transition may be the key to finding balance in what remains an engaged and productive life.

It's a big mindset shift to think of yourself first, but it's critical if you want to thrive. Your brain will battle with you, throwing up all the reasons why you shouldn't:

- *I don't want to be selfish.*
- *I can't stand 'me-focused' people.*
- *I'd rather just support others from the background.*
- *Does that mean I'll be self-obsessed?*

The truth is, you can't truly understand what you deeply desire until you make yourself a priority. Anything less than that will keep you hitched to someone else's wagon: "I'm going to do this because it will still allow me to be there for the kids." It sounds reasonable, but are you really helping them, or are you simply hiding behind them?

It's a service to let go and give others the opportunity to stand on their own 2 feet. If you're struggling to elevate yourself to the top of the pile, start by identifying the places where you are over-servicing.

I drove my kids to and from school for way too long. "It's our special time together," I told myself. That special time together also meant that I condensed an 8-hour work day into 4, with all the stress that brought. But this choice didn't just impact on me. I stole a sense of adventure and independence from my kids that was critical once they reached a certain age. Instead, I could have delegated more and asked for help. It doesn't mean you don't care anymore. Those who love you will fully support it when you give back to yourself.

"I've always wanted to be a health coach," my 55-year-old friend said at lunch one day. We were all excited, because we'd been wanting her to leave her dead-end and stressful job for ages.

We chimed in with our advice: "Yes, you should totally do that! There's an 18-month course you can start next week. I can totally see you doing that!"

"I need to wait until my youngest son has left school. Plus, my husband has just changed jobs. Oh, and the team at work may not cope with my decreased focus. Besides, I probably feel at my least confident at the moment."

She was a powerful force of a woman, and we could all see she was ready, but sometimes fear hides behind the burdens of responsibility. We're scared of what it would be like to put ourselves first, so we prolong the phase of putting ourselves last.

Don't pull away from the call to be powerful and fierce, joyful and bold.

Our brains lean towards maintaining the status quo. It feels more comfortable and takes less energy to repeat the same patterns over and over again, but these circles will get smaller and smaller as you age. Delaying tactics only postpone your happiness, and resentment builds as you watch everyone else rise.

No-one can do this for you. It's up to you to step into Wise Woman energy. When you are living as the best version of yourself, you'll automatically become the best partner, mother, friend, worker and neighbour. It's a win-win for everyone, but don't be surprised if others initially don't like it. When you bring your power back to yourself, the whole grid feels a shift. The people who became accustomed to using your over-compensating energy suddenly feel alert to the fact that something is missing. They can become needy or demanding, but stay true to yourself, knowing that this will pass and benefit everyone in the long run.

What's your new narrative?

These are just a few things that may be influencing your approach to your second half. Hopefully they've given you much to reflect on, and possibly highlighted mindsets, stereotypes, myths or patterns that form a narrative that holds you back. Now is the time to rewrite that narrative into something that gets you running onto the field to play your second half with all the wisdom, energy and grace of your accumulated years.

The way to live big is to play a different game in the second half. Put yourself first, and follow your desires and curiosity.

Years of conditioning can be hard to change. It starts with awareness, then small habitual changes. Try the following exercises to limber up your mind, before you dive into the coming chapters to enhance your physical, mental, emotional and spiritual health.

1. My narrative

a. *Think of the words 'middle-aged woman', and write for 5 minutes (completely unfiltered) on the narrative that comes straight to your mind. Include it all, no matter whether you like it or not.*

....
....
....
....
....
....
....
....

b. What's the new narrative you'd like to embed?

....
....
....
....
....
....
....
....
....
....
....
....
....
....

- *For one day, fully embrace the new narrative.*
- *Ask yourself, "What would the Wise Woman do, how would she think, act and feel?" Then do what arises.*
- *Adopt a Wise Woman mantra and say it to yourself in the mirror every morning. For example, "I am strong, I am sovereign, I am wise." Pick your own few lines from your new narrative.*

2. Top of the pile

It might take some effort to reconnect to your own needs again. They probably haven't received much airtime for a while. Pick up a journal and reconnect with yourself by asking some of the following questions and writing what comes to mind:

- *What are the biggest needs I have right now?*
- *What are the biggest desires I have right now?*
- *If I were to truly put myself first, what's one thing I'd do differently?*
- *Where am I over-servicing others, or using one of my perceived responsibilities, to stay small?*

3. Re-energise

Start practising some self-care.

- *How would you look after a queen? Believe me, queens aren't jumping out of bed, looking after everyone else and racing frazzled into their days. They spend a large portion of their day preparing themselves to show up in the world. And they have boundaries!*
- *What would it look like to truly nurture yourself? Do one thing every day. Have a massage, buy yourself flowers, light a candle, take some deep breaths, have a bath.*
- *Ask yourself every day: "What does the most important person in my life need right now?" Then make that a priority.*
- *Ask yourself: "What boundaries do I need to put in place, so I'm not exhausted and can be at my best?"*

Matt: While the transition for men is certainly different, the common denominator here is that we are all confronting change. Men and women, we both need to challenge ourselves by asking whether we want to fall into the antiquated stereotypes of ageing, or step into the unknown and embrace being confident, powerful and wise.

Susan: Couldn't have said it better, Matt. Now give us the unspoken men's business.

Section 3
Unspoken Men's Business

Chapter 12

Men's Talk

Now it was my turn to lift the lid on men. I reflected on a key difference I'd noticed in Susan's stories: *One thing you women have going for you is how much you share with each other.* If I'm honest, what I was really thinking was I'd love to be a fly on the wall at one of her girl's lunches!

Susan: A lot of it would bore you because when a group of 50-something-year-old women gather, it's not so different to girls catching up in their 20s. We compliment each other on clothes and shoes, find out where everyone went for their holidays, and share tips on the best new restaurants and bars. But as the hours pass by and the drinks flow, the conversation inevitably turns to men.

Before you break out in a cold sweat every time a woman departs for lunch with her friends, I'd better make a few things clear. These aren't big bitch sessions about men. We talk about men to try and understand them. That's probably one of the big differences between men and women. When women are confused, troubled or don't understand something, they take it to other women and we sort it out together. We don't struggle silently, trying to find the answer by ourselves. Asking for help from our girlfriends is one of our superpowers. In fact, many a marriage has been saved by these girl's lunches.

Matt: That's reassuring!

Susan: Women are puzzled about why men don't talk to us about their problems. When they do, we see it as a really positive thing. When they don't, we see the issue anyway, so staying silent does more damage than good. One of the biggest misunderstandings between men and women is that we see your vulnerability as strength. There is nothing more attractive to a woman than a man who can be self-reflective and express his emotions. Men seem to think we will see that as weak, but it's quite the opposite. I don't necessarily want a man having more regular meltdowns than I do, or become so caught up in his emotions that he gets nothing done, but that's not what we're talking about here. We are talking about conscious men who have enough confidence to express what they feel, rather than hiding it. There is nothing more unattractive than a shut-down man who is hiding his insecurities by inflating his ego.

Matt: Don't hold back, Susan! I'm kidding. As always, you make a very valid point. When a group of men get together, we usually talk about sport, politics or current affairs. Keeping our unspoken men's business locked up inside is not only a recipe for disaster in relationships, it's a disaster for our own health and happiness. We have other superpowers, but we would benefit a lot by learning how to open up more and ask for help.

My goal in this chapter is to explore what holds us back, and to help men see that it's better to air stuff in healthy ways, otherwise it can be messy and destructive.

Susan: How did you discover that, Matt?

Matt: Like you, Susan, I'm going to start a few years back and share my journey of self-discovery.

I walked out of the Love Beans Café in Sydney in 2014, digesting the news that I had been sacked from my job as Head Coach of the New Zealand Warriors. In a complete state of denial, I couldn't understand how this was happening. Just the year before, the club had offered me a contract extension, and discussed making me the Non-Executive Director of Football Operations. Then, only 5 weeks into the season, with a record of 2 wins and 3 losses, I was let go.

When I reflect on that moment 12 years later, I realise the club's decision was completely justified, not because I wasn't working hard enough or didn't understand my craft as well as anyone in the sport, but because I had withdrawn into myself. I had created distance in my relationships with players, coaches and staff in a profession where connecting with people is paramount. It was my job to provide feedback to improve the team, therefore it was essential that I make each person feel safe and valued. But I had prioritised strategy, structure and future planning over personal connections. As someone with a strong understanding of these principles and a lot of mentoring experience, how did this happen?

You don't get to the second half of life without facing challenges and trauma.

I look back at that time in my life with some self-compassion and can see the factors at play. I'd been in high-pressure positions, where scrutiny and consequences were constant, for a long time. The additional load of getting divorced and adapting to not seeing my daughters regularly took its toll. The final straw came after a relationship with someone I genuinely loved broke down. The accumulated stress manifested into an autoimmune disease called polymyalgia rheumatica. In short, the body's immune system mistakenly attacks the lining of joints and surrounding tissue, leading to inflammation. It impacts the blood vessels and causes acute pain. Being a stereotypical Australian male, I didn't tell anyone, and quietly injected myself with steroids twice a day for the pain.

This is not a 'poor me' story. If I were giving advice to a mate going through the same experience, I'd tell him to seek support and focus on the important things in life and work, as that's where healing comes from.

Ultimately, my decision was to remove myself from familiar environments and travel to Cambodia, where I rode a bike through the backfields of that amazing country. Eventually, I took responsibility for what had happened, instead of blaming others. Blame takes away your power to make changes, so this was the start of addressing my situation. The next part of the process, which took at least a year, involved overcoming denial. I needed to learn from what had occurred so I wouldn't make the same mistake again. As the saying goes: *Mistakes happen, but the same mistake twice is a decision.* You don't get to the second half of life without facing challenges and trauma.

Rest assured, just because something has happened once doesn't mean it won't happen again. While most of these experiences can't be framed as positive, we need to find learning and beauty in them, so we can continue to grow. By doing so, we can turn these experiences into wisdom, and that's what will carry us more smoothly through future challenges. It's about transforming pain into a source of strength and insight, and ensuring that our personal growth also benefits those around us.

Chapter 13

Redefining Outdated Norms

I continued to reflect on Susan's profound insights into the difficulties women face as they transition through life. It was eye-opening for me, especially as a father to 4 daughters. Her words pushed me to confront my own biases and acknowledge the immense contributions of the women in my life, including my mother and sisters. She also made me think hard about the myths of modern masculinity.

Matt: I've grappled with restrictive stereotypes that have long plagued men. Traditional ideals of manhood have been hit pretty hard by evolving gender roles, and there's no doubt it can lead to confusion, internal conflict and mental health issues. Dismantling outdated notions and exploring what it truly means to be a man (or woman) today is long overdue.

Research has shown time and time again just how damaging rigid gender norms can be to our mental health and overall wellbeing. Women are constantly bombarded with unrealistic beauty standards, which leads to problems like low self-esteem and body dysmorphia. I'm also really aware of how widespread the messaging is to women that they should keep their mouths shut, as if their voice doesn't matter. They seem to face a never-ending battle to gain control over their own lives.

Men are expected to be strong, emotionless beings, and that leaves them feeling alone and unable to express their true feelings. No wonder they face higher rates of depression, anxiety, substance abuse and even suicide.[6] It's like they're drowning in toxic masculinity that leaves no room for vulnerability or genuine emotion. Who says strength means being emotionless? And who says femininity is synonymous with weakness? We need to redefine what it means to be a man and a woman, and acknowledge that there's a huge spectrum of identities beyond those binary categories.

Why can't we create safe spaces where individuals can freely explore their gender identity? Whether through therapy, support groups or online communities, providing a place where people can be seen, heard and validated is crucial. Our communities benefit when we can all be our authentic selves, without fear or judgement. When we take a long hard look at the damage rigid gender norms are doing, it's clear that our world is a lesser place because of the pressure to conform to old societal norms. These norms aren't some holy truths. They're just made-up social constructs that have been passed down for way too long. When we embrace the beautiful, diverse tapestry of human beings, our willing connection to each other becomes the foundation upon which we all learn, grow and thrive.

So, what's all this got to do with winning in the second half? I think about it this way. In my second half, I can finally stand back and see the bigger picture with a degree of wisdom I didn't have in my youth. I was too focused on my own achievements back then, but now I feel a strong drive to make

---

6 - See References 6.

a difference, using what I have learnt and the experiences I have accumulated.

Older people are often accused of being grumpy, stuck in their ways and irrelevant to the next generation, but I don't buy that. We can change the world, but we've got to change ourselves first.

We need to acknowledge our own biases and confront how we might be perpetuating these harmful constructs. It's uncomfortable and it's challenging, but it's also incredibly rewarding and invigorating. I think this is what the second half of the game is all about.

Susan: What a manifesto, Matt! You're clearly passionate, but you're also compassionate, which is a powerful combination. I agree that we all have so much to offer in our second half. For some people, that might be teaching their grandkids something they'll never learn in school; for others, it might be creating a massive movement for global change. I also agree that change starts with ourselves. Tell me what you think that looks like for men.

We can change the world, but we've got to change ourselves first.

Matt: Understanding the male journey requires unravelling the conditioning that has shaped our behaviour for millennia. At our core, all humans crave safety and belonging, which are needs ingrained in our DNA from our days as cave dwellers. Back then, trust and community were essential for survival, with men often taking on the role of protector and provider, while women bore reproductive risks. This primal instinct to safeguard our tribe can be a meaningful role when aligned with a sense of service and genuine purpose. We'll willingly use up every ounce of our energy to fight off threats, build shelter and find resources for those within our circle. When we get rewarded for those efforts, we'll work twice as hard to do it all again. It is incredibly fulfilling when channelled productively.

Looking at the state of the world, however, it's obvious that this ancient mindset can take men down the wrong path. Some world leaders epitomise the pitfalls of unchecked ego and outdated masculinity. They find their worthiness in dominating others, rather than protecting them, and in acquiring privilege for themselves, rather than providing for others. This impulse to assert power over others only perpetuates harm and division.

I grew up in a society that constantly hammered us with rigid beliefs about what it meant to be a man. From an early age, I witnessed the destructive consequences of toxic masculinity firsthand. Men were supposed to be tough, dominant and emotionally void, which led to a suppression of their true feelings. It also perpetuated harmful behaviours. Men have been trapped in these suffocating stereotypes and expectations for far too long. It stifles their true potential and wreaks havoc on their emotional wellbeing. Future generations of men deserve a more authentic vision of masculinity.

As I grew older (this is one of the beautiful things about moving into your second half), I started questioning these societal norms, realising that true strength lies in vulnerability. Emotional intelligence is just as vital as physical prowess, but finding that balance demands that we break the chains and explore new definitions of masculinity. It must be a narrative that allows men to embrace their authentic selves and unleash their untapped power.

In my mission to redefine masculinity, I've delved deep into extensive research, seeking guidance from psychologists, sociologists and countless experts in the field. The findings paint a compelling picture: masculinity doesn't have to be synonymous with power-hungry aggression and dominance. Instead, it's all about breaking free from the suffocating clutches of traditional gender roles and embracing vulnerability, emotional intelligence, empathy and compassion.

Men should feel free to express their emotions; to shed tears, to laugh with joy and to dive headfirst into true love. We must be encouraged to seek support when we need it, and to reject the notion that vulnerability is a weakness. By doing so, we can create a society where men not only find happiness within themselves, but also become more connected, empathetic individuals.

But it doesn't stop there. Redefining masculinity means squarely addressing the impact of toxic masculinity on relationships and intimacy. These old expectations have prevented men from forming deep emotional connections. Instead, they make us keep others at arm's length, while we remain emotionally shuttered. We must create the breathing space for men to build healthier, more satisfying relationships founded on trust, emotional closeness and mutual support.

I'd love every man to take their own journey into redefining masculinity. Reflecting on my own evolution, I've found that true strength lies not in domination, but in empathy and compassion. Let's be clear, this doesn't mean casting aside every aspect of traditional masculinity. It's about broadening our understanding of manhood, and recognising that there is no one-size-fits-all definition. Men can still be strong, physically capable and assertive, but they can also express vulnerability, show compassion and be emotionally available. As you pointed out, Susan, women want us to be their grounding force. They don't want us to become them, but they do want us to share in the entire spectrum of human emotion and traits, without fear or judgement.

Susan: I think that balance is probably hard for men to get their head around, let alone master.

It's your emotional connection that will be your greatest legacy as a man.

Matt: And I can hear some guys dry-retching and accusing me of skipping through fields wearing rose-coloured glasses. Old Matt would have done the same thing, before I realised how much our conditioning numbs us to really connecting with life. This isn't about being 'Positive Pete'; it's about making the harder decisions to enjoy life. Try exercising, rather than sitting on the lounge; cook a healthy meal, rather than going to Macca's; learn something new, rather than watching repeats of *Friends*; or find a way to forgive someone, rather than spending a lifetime in anger. All of these things are scientifically proven to improve your health. I'm not suggesting you skip around the fields singing love songs while eating organic salad and learning quantum physics your whole life. There are plenty of approachable actions that elevate your wellbeing most of the time, and still let you be a bloke who says 'fuck', has a beer and occasionally gets the shits.

If you want to have an awesome second half of life, especially with all the unprecedented change coming our way, the virtues of empathy, vulnerability and willingness to learn will never lose their relevance. This journey of self-discovery requires confronting our deepest fears and insecurities, and challenging narratives ingrained since childhood. But it's a journey worth taking, because shedding the armour of masculinity opens us up to a world of possibility and freedom. It's your emotional connection that will be your greatest legacy as a man.

The journey requires some real male grit, so keep those rose-coloured glasses handy!

Chapter 14

Rules for Life

Susan looked a bit concerned. "Matt, many of my friends sense that the men in their life are going through something at this stage, but men seem determined to conceal it and go deep into themselves."

Not for the first time, Susan was revealing how well women pick up on the unspoken stuff that we men think we're hiding. "Yes, we're good at that," I admitted, "but the 'strong, silent type' is often a powder keg waiting to explode. At least that's how it was for me."

Matt: I was 55 years old. I was in denial about my situation, fabricating lies to myself and others about what was actually happening. Physically, I had a knee that was caving in after more than 10 surgeries. Mentally, I was experiencing deep brain fog, which I silently put down to head knocks from playing professional rugby league. Emotionally, I was feeling numb after coming out of my third long-term failed relationship. I'd given up on finding love, and then I lost my mother.

Those personal challenges were compounded by blows in my business life. I had to step back from a job I loved due to a family situation, and my business encountered some major setbacks coming out of COVID. Throughout it all, I was mentoring individuals with psychological injuries, helping them to reclaim their wellbeing and return to a functional life. I was providing individual leadership and life coaching for corporate executives, offering emotional resilience wellbeing presentations, and holding down a role as a mindset, leadership and culture coordinator.

I was seriously fucked up. Having the knowledge and practical understanding of techniques to deal with my situation did allow me to create some respite, but the innate human response in these situations is fight, flight or freeze. I didn't become aggressive, nor did I escape, however 'freeze' certainly goes close to explaining my behaviour. I showed up to work every day, engaged with those I cared for, socialised enough not to concern anyone, but I slowly (and unconsciously) engaged less with normal life. My desire to be in environments I love evaporated. Connecting with friends and family became a task I performed just enough to appease them.

The subconscious programming in my head was telling me:

- You're too old to get the job you want.
- There's no way you're going to meet your soulmate at this age.
- Mate, your kids have enough going on; just leave them be.
- Your colleagues don't give a shit; they think you're past it.

These are just some of the lies I was telling myself to validate my poor engagement with life. Even though I'd had an amazing life leading up to that point, all my measures of success and purpose were things I assumed were suddenly beyond my capabilities. I'd convinced myself all these problems were because of the date on my birth certificate; but the truth was, I hadn't taken the time to figure out what I really wanted in my life.

Susan: So how did you get help with this?

Matt: Like a lot of men, I prided myself on being self-sufficient, but I had the good sense to turn to a book. One of my favourite books, *The Four Agreements* by Don Miguel Ruiz, has profoundly impacted my life. I've read it at least twice a year for the last decade, and it motivated me to develop my 'rules for life'. Their purpose is to accelerate a healthy transition into the second half of life, and move me beyond the stereotype of the grumpy, tired and redundant old man.

My 4 rules may encourage other men to redefine the narrative they wish to live by in their second half:

1. **I Am Worthy.** I'm worthy to receive opportunities, love and other amazing experiences. I am also worthy to support others who want to create a better life, by sharing my wisdom and experiences. This rule was a response to insecurities about being past my use-by date and people not respecting me, because the knowledge I had to share was redundant.

2. **I Don't Know.** For much of my life as a male leader in sport and business I thought it was my responsibility to know everything. It inhibited my ability to learn new things and, most importantly, prevented others from sharing their wisdom with me. It's in what we don't know that learning and new

opportunities exist. If we already knew it, we would have already experienced it. I love saying "I don't know" these days!

3. **Don't Complain.** Not even to yourself. It wasn't until I activated this mantra in my life that I realised how much time I spent in my head negatively assessing situations, both real and made-up. Not only was it the poorest use of time, ruminating over things that never actually eventuated, it also put me in a state that prevented me being productive, and it stole my enjoyment in life. I wish I could say this was an easy habit to break, but consistent conscious accountability has allowed me to improve my productivity and experiences in life. I have done one-on-one coaching with thousands of people, and it appears I am not the only one who has inhibited themselves with this unconstructive choice of thoughts. We are designed to look for threat, and if we don't have a process to snap us out of it, we get stuck in a very negative loop.

4. **Become an Expert in Yourself.** My job as a leader was to know my job, create systems and structures to allow others to do their job, and know how each individual responded in certain situations. Many of us have expertise in the external world, but how much expertise do we have in ourselves? When we see a friend or a loved one, our first question is, "Hi, how are you going?" But how often do you ask yourself this question, and how aware are you of the answer? The truth for most of us is that it's not until the shit hits the fan that we check in with ourselves, and the answer then is something like, "I have to change my

whole life" or "I just didn't see this coming". This rule has made a big difference to many people I have coached, as well as to me. Check in with yourself once a day by asking, "How am I going and why?" It creates genuine self-awareness that allows you to tap into your own wisdom and resolve challenges. When you can't find an answer, turn to Rule 2 and seek the advice of a mentor, a clinician or someone you trust.

Susan: These are great rules. I might steal some of them. How have they helped you?

Matt: I'm 60 years old as this book goes to print, and I know I'm seen as old by many people, but that doesn't mean I need to embrace this stereotype. I feel vibrant and healthy, I believe I have important contributions to make, and I know I am worthy to receive the goodness of life. While this is much easier to write than to act on every day, it's my decision to make.

When the inevitable obstacles of ageing do show up, I intend to see that resistance as if it's an additional weight on a barbell, increasing my opportunity for growth. Yeah, you might be thinking, *Mate, your optimism is a touch unrealistic.* But it is my choice to feel and think this way. It might seem easier to be pessimistic, but when you believe that your response is your choice, it puts you in control of your life.

I have been blessed to spend a lot of time with Paralympians, war veterans, retired police and crime victims, all of whom have every right to be consumed by their challenges. Instead, their response has been to use their experiences to improve their life and inspire others.

While most of us aren't coming out of the same acute experiences, we all have the opportunity to choose how we respond to life's inevitable adversities. Old and grumpy or ageing and uplifting? You choose.

Chapter 15

The Power of Self-Awareness

Now we were getting to a topic I'm super passionate about.

Matt: One of my key teaching points to individuals and groups around mental and emotional wellbeing is self-awareness. I suspect women might be better at this then most men. To make the lesson simple, I always ask, "What do you do when you have a rock in your shoe?"

Susan: Obviously the answer is, "I take it out."

Matt: Then I ask, "What happens if you ignore it?" We all know the pain gets worse. If you keep ignoring it, the pain will move from discomfort to agony.

Your mental and emotional states are the same. If you start off being frustrated by something, and your conditioning as a middle-aged man says you should harden up and have a cup of concrete, that frustration escalates to anger, and ultimately to rage. Suddenly you find yourself screaming at someone or getting aggressive for no justifiable reason.

The most effective way to resolve this is through self-awareness, by asking yourself: "Why am I frustrated, and what do I need to do?" This may sound simple, but in my experience, it has proved super effective for the thousands of people with whom I have shared it. The challenge for many men is that they don't have a lot of experience paying attention to how they feel, which may explain why we are over-represented in mental health statistics.

Fellas, we've never really been encouraged to explore our emotional depth and sit with our feelings, but if you are like most of the blokes I know, you have emotional baggage that's been eating away at you for ages. Now, you can take the time-honoured approach and go down the pub to indulge in the required number of beverages to dull the problem, but you know it's not going away. Equally, I'm sure you're aware that this practice is not enhancing your health or your relationships.

So, what harm is there in trying something different? Sitting quietly and stilling your mind, walking in nature or visualising desired outcomes are very simple actions, but they do require that you make a different choice. That can be difficult but hey, you're a strong guy. At the very worst, you'll be able to say you tried it before dismissing it. At best, it will work, and those things that used to eat away at you become things of the past. Surely the potential to reset your life has got to be worth a crack?

Susan: And I guess as you start to slow down in the second half, you have more time to prioritise these things. Do men do this though? Most I know get even busier as space starts to open up for them. Can men just stop and enjoy the stillness of the moment? That's a key part of self-reflection for me.

Matt: I've watched a couple of mates, high-achieving alpha males, make difficult transformations from working minimum 12-hour days running massive organisations, to becoming stay-at-home dads and adventurers with their partners. I've also witnessed some of my most functional friends in constant conflict with their partners about taking opportunities to enjoy life now. If asked, "What's the key difference between them?" my answer would be self-awareness.

Deep within the male subconscious lies the belief that significance is directly tied to our ability to support loved ones – not just while we're here, but through what we leave behind after we depart this planet. This fear of becoming redundant is part of the DNA associated with the protector role in the tribe, and it's reinforced by stereotypes and role models throughout our lives. While it may not make much sense when scrutinised, there is a genuine fear of irrelevance, and therefore a strong motivation to be a key figure in relationships. For men, that usually means physical contributions, even when women are desperately craving emotional connection.

The ones who are able to pivot towards connection and make changes to their lives, so that they are cultivating their relationships, are the ones who've overcome denial by engaging seriously in their self-awareness efforts.

I had a client who was the owner and CEO of a company with a $10-billion turnover, employing more than 4,000 staff. Watching him slowly shift from a ridiculous workload to prioritising his life, wife and family was fascinating. He made time for shared experiences, fun and the interests of others. Some might say it's easier for a rich guy, but having worked with many affluent men in one-on-one coaching, I can attest that wealth often comes with its own set of miseries.

Similarly, my mate quit his job to work in his wife's café. Although financially on the opposite end of the spectrum to my client, his motives and challenges were almost identical. Both men decided it was time to shift their priorities to their partners. While the decision made complete sense to them, transformation isn't a one-off decision or a habit that can be ingrained easily. Self-awareness is an everyday job, but the tougher the challenge you overcome, the more rewarding the result.

Susan: It's really good to hear these examples, because women often feel that men are too driven by finances. It sounds something like this: "My husband is miserable. He hates his job and it affects his mood. Our relationship is really suffering, but I don't think he can see it. I have tried to support him to find other jobs, but he won't leave because the job is highly paid. He won't take a $5,000 pay cut. We always said we'd move to the beach, and I know that doesn't fix everything, but I believe we'd be a lot happier there. We could sell one of our 3 investment properties and live where we really want instead. But he says he won't go backwards and that we need to work hard for another 5 years to add to our property portfolio. I've been quite depressed the last 6 months, and it's affecting our relationship, sex drive and everything. I fear I won't be here in 5 years."

Time and time again, you can see the hard lesson is not being learnt. I had a partner who was so fixated on paying off the mortgage, but the day never came because the relationship ended before the mortgage did. Women are confused by this prioritisation, but as you've explained really well, men tend to judge themselves more on achievement, their mission and their provider status. I think in the second half, sometimes you need to go backwards to go forwards.

Self-awareness is an everyday job.

Matt: Yes, and partners need to have good conversations, to reconcile how they can prioritise happiness for both. Our survey showed that men in the second half placed a greater priority on finances, whereas women prioritised travel and adventures. This could become a thorn in the relationship, if a compromise isn't reached.

Chapter 16

Busting Myths

Susan was listening intently, but I could see she had questions. "What's on your mind?" I asked.

Susan: Matt, I've gathered so many questions about men during my girls' lunches, and you've answered some of them. But here is a situation that comes up a lot. I'd appreciate your perspective on it. Like I said earlier, women talk about this stuff because they want to save their marriages, not because they want to criticise men.

Matt: Okay, give it to me, Susan. I'll see what I can do.

Susan: A woman might start with, "Something is wrong with him. It's like he's a different person." Of course, being a woman, she's asked him what's wrong. "He says it's nothing and I'm being paranoid, but he's drinking more, sleeping less, spending money like it's going out of fashion, and he always seems to be miles away in his head. He's got a really short fuse and has angry outbursts all the time. And he's stopped wanting to have sex."

My first assumption would be that he's having an affair, but what do you think, Matt?

Matt: Classic men's unspoken business, but it could be any of those issues and it's not always an affair, Susan. In fact, this reminds me of one of the things that men never talk about, even with each other.

Not so long ago, I was sitting on the couch watching the cricket, completely absorbed in the match. Suddenly an ad popped up about 'hitting the ball hard through the covers'. While I was trying to process what they meant, the next message was, 'No quick singles required, you can stay at the crease and bat for hours.' Then it dawned on me; this wasn't a cricket ad at all, it was a cleverly disguised ad for Viagra. All I could think was: *Well, that's an interesting way to advertise erectile dysfunction and sell the blue pill.* It made me cringe and laugh all at once.

Susan, you've shared your insights into menopause, a mysterious world that's rarely shared with us men and, when it is, usually has us diving under the table to avoid being caught in the crossfire. What we really don't hear much about is how men in their second half of life experience their own set of quiet battles around declining sexual drive, virility and intimacy. Not only do men not share this with women, we don't even talk about it with each other. It really is 'unspoken', but I think it's about time we gave it a little air.

As we age, physical issues that might have been silent in our younger days can rear their heads. High blood pressure and plaque in our arteries can reduce blood flow throughout the body. In fact, erectile dysfunction is often the first warning sign of cardiovascular disease. The next risk factor includes common lifestyle changes as we age, such as reduced exercise levels, diet short cuts, and indulging in a few more beers than we should. And then there's the factor we can't control, which is the natural decline in testosterone as we age.

But it doesn't stop with the physical factors. Our self-esteem can take a hit, and we wonder if we'll ever feel the same energy or desire again. While most of us in the second half of life don't want to create more little humans, we still want to feel like, well, ourselves. But the worry and the fear that we've lost it can become self-fulfilling.

As much as we want to talk about this, we really don't because it's embarrassing. Most blokes would rather discuss anything other than a decline in their masculinity. If we do talk about it with mates, it won't go beyond a few awkward jokes. But because our partners are usually the first ones to notice changes, they are often the first ones to raise the subject. Now, the male ego has a funny way of handling such situations. Denial is often the first defence: "I'm fine, it's just stress," or "It's nothing, really". We try to shut down the conversation, but deep down we know there's something going on.

If you do see your doctor (probably because your partner insisted), that's another hurdle. Sure, it's supposed to be a safe space, but it's hard to admit this challenge, even to a professional. If you're lucky, your doctor will run checks on your overall health and identify whether your issues are the symptom of a wider vascular problem. That could save your life.

But your doctor might just hand over a prescription for the famous little blue pill. For a time, it may work well; but the pill addresses the symptoms, not the root cause. If low testosterone levels and high blood pressure from poor lifestyle habits are left unaddressed, the pill's effects will fade over time.

We try to shut down the conversation, but deep down we know there's something going on.

But here's the good news: there are simple lifestyle changes that can have a profound impact on your health, your intimacy and your sense of self. We share many of them throughout this book, but here's a quick summary of what you can do to get back out on the cricket pitch and 'knock the middle stump out of the ground'!

1. **Eat Whole Foods:** This one's pretty straightforward. Get rid of the processed junk. Processed foods (especially those high in sugar, corn syrup and soy) mess with your hormones, particularly testosterone. Focus on nutrient-dense, whole foods like wild-caught fish, grass-fed beef, pasture-raised chicken, eggs, avocados, nuts and berries. These simple additions can help boost your vitality.

2. **Cut Back on Alcohol:** A drink here and there is fine, but too much alcohol wreaks havoc on hormone production, testicular function and even sleep. It also raises cortisol (the stress hormone), which signals your body that it's under threat. Not the message you want your body getting if you want to enjoy intimacy.

3. **Seek Personal Support:** Here's the big thing no-one really talks about: being a man means you're often expected to be the provider and protector. When that internal identity is challenged, it can eat away at you. That emotional battle is one many men never share, and holding it all in puts your body into a perpetual state of stress. Constantly dealing with cortisol and adrenaline might not have the immediate physical consequences of being chased by a tiger, but over time, it takes a toll on your health, including your testosterone levels. Speaking to a counsellor or someone you trust can help you manage those feelings. Talking about it helps you regain not just your health, but also your confidence.

4. **Exercise:** You've heard it before and I'll say it again. Whether it's lifting weights, walking or swimming, keeping your body active is one of the best ways to maintain testosterone levels, improve mood and boost self-esteem. A healthy body leads to a healthy mind, and a healthy sex life.

5. **Practice:** Yes, practice. Intimacy benefits from being nurtured and worked on. And no, I'm not talking about 'performance' in the traditional sense, but rather taking the time to connect with your partner or yourself, consistently. Like anything, the more you practice, the better you get at it. Just don't overdo it – like all things, overtraining can cause injury. I'm sure you understand what I'm getting at!

Susan: That was very insightful, Matt. I'll stop jumping to the conclusion that every man who's acting withdrawn is having an affair! Do you have any other practical tips for redefining modern masculinity?

Matt: Yes, like you suggested to women, it starts by challenging the myths that might be limiting your vision for your second half. I'd like guys to put pen to paper and try some of the suggestions below.

Busting Male Myths

Read each myth and answer the questions honestly. You can journal your thoughts for greater effect, and it's useful to come back later when you want to remind yourself of insights you gained during this exercise. Then answer the 3 questions at the end.

Myth 1: I'm Too Old to Start Something New

- *Do you find yourself using age as an excuse to avoid new opportunities or changes?*
- *Are there specific interests or endeavours you've hesitated to pursue, due to age-related beliefs?*
- *How might stepping out of your comfort zone positively impact your wellbeing?*

Myth 2: Real Men Don't Show Emotions

- *Have you ever felt pressured to hide your emotions to conform to societal expectations?*
- *In what ways has suppressing emotions affected your health or relationships?*
- *How can acknowledging and expressing emotions contribute to a healthier and more fulfilling life?*

Myth 3: Physical Fitness Is Only for the Young

- *Are there physical activities you've avoided, due to perceived limitations or embarrassment?*
- *How do you currently view the relationship between exercise and overall wellbeing?*
- *What steps can you take to incorporate suitable physical activities into your routine?*

Myth 4: I've Earnt the Right to Have the Shits Because I'm Right

- *Have you ever found yourself in a situation where expressing frustration overshadowed your message?*
- *How might listening without judgement enhance your ability to communicate effectively?*
- *What steps can you take to ensure your experiences contribute to constructive conversations?*

Myth 5: I'm No Longer Relevant in the Workplace

- *Have you encountered situations where age was perceived as a barrier to relevance at work?*
- *How can the wealth of your experience be an asset in your professional environment?*
- *What steps can you take to embrace new learning and stay cognitively engaged?*

Myth 6: I Should Be Financially Secure by Now

- *Have you felt pressured by societal expectations regarding financial stability?*

- *How can you redefine your financial goals based on your desires, rather than preconceived notions?*
- *What steps can you take to create a plan that aligns with your life aspirations?*

Question 1: *Reflecting on these myths, which ones resonate with you the most, and why?*

Question 2: *In what ways can challenging and letting go of these myths contribute to a more meaningful, healthy and enjoyable life?*

Question 3: *What specific actions can you take to create self-awareness and address these myths in your own life?*

Ageing Reprogramming

It can be a real challenge to combat the subconscious programming that says 'old equals past your prime'. But if you can choose 1 or 2 things to defy that prediction, you can reprogram your ageing mindset.

As a kid, my ability to remember names was terrible. I'd meet someone and literally a minute later, their name was gone from my brain. I'd laugh it off and use the word 'mate' for everyone. As I approached the second half, I'd laugh it off with, "Ah, you're just getting old, Matt."

At 60, I have made the decision that I'm going to be better than ever at remembering names. So, now when I meet someone new, I repeat their name 4 times in my head, and attach a rhythm and rhyme to it. For example, Susan, Susan, Susan, Susan, she's choosin', cruisin' and boozin'.

Guess what? It works, and I'm better at remembering names than ever.

Susan: Great tip Matt, but I'm really worried that you associate me with cruising and boozing!

Matt: Ha! I thought you'd like that one.

I've got one more set of practical suggestions. Something men in the second half struggle with a lot is self-love. For many of us, the saying 'you love yourself' was an insult, implying that you were self-absorbed and had no humility. Men's inability to love themselves sits at the foundation of their over-representation in the mental health epidemic.

For many, this is not only a secret they keep from others, it's something they've probably never seriously contemplated. First Nations people understand that you can't give what you don't have. I think this is essential learning to really thrive in the second half of life. It is a very simple concept to understand: if you want to love others and love life, you need to love yourself.

Men's inability to love themselves sits at the foundation of their over-representation in the mental health epidemic.

Redefining Love (Give to Get)
My 5 fundamentals for self-love are:

1. **Self-Compassion:** Be kind to myself, and be aware when my internal criticism mechanism starts. Cut it off at the pass.

2. **Meditation:** Give my brain a break from continuous thinking, and connect with my inner self to grow awareness and self-worth.

3. **Journaling:** This reminds me what I value in life and in myself. It is a record of how I want to be and what I want in life.

4. **Gratitude:** Remind myself of the amazing things I do have in my life.

5. **Forgiveness:** Let go of self-criticism and judgement of others. Forgive others – it doesn't mean I think some things are right, it means I love myself too much to carry the load of other people's stuff.

These are daily practices that I focus on at particular times in my day: upon waking, when driving, working out and before bed. Give them a try or make up your own self-love fundamentals.
These conversations with Susan really helped me face some of the myths and stereotypes facing men and women in the second half. It's crucial that we change the way we think, and actively choose our own narrative. Once you've done that, it's

time to dive deeper into the tools that can make your second half the best half of your life.

Susan: So where do you want to start Matt – physical, mental, emotional or spiritual tools?

Matt: Let's get physical!

Section 4
Let's Get Physical

Chapter 17

Decomplicating the Physical

Susan was smiling as she took me on a trip down memory lane.

Susan: You know, Matt, I remember watching you on TV when you played with the Dragons NRL team.

Matt: Well, I'm very glad you saw me in my prime, Susan. I hope it was early in my career when I was invincible! Unfortunately, my strongest memory from watching myself on TV comes from 2021. The footage shows me as a coach warming the team up, but I was hobbling from one activity to another. It was shocking and embarrassing. I had to ask myself, *Is that really me?*

My mates had been giving me grief for ages about my deteriorating knee, constantly telling me, "You need to get that fixed." The other players on the team loved to refer to my birth certificate, suggesting age was the cause of my problems. You can just imagine it.

Susan: Why didn't you do something about it?

Matt: It was the 'she'll be right' syndrome, the denial many men have about ageing and the necessary adjustments we should be making. Couple that with my genuine reluctance to take time off and be a burden on others. I ignored the problem.

The result was overcompensation by my good knee and misalignment in my hips. I'm just one of thousands of examples among my male friends, whether they're former athletes, CEOs sitting at a desk all day, or tradies without healthy lifestyle habits.

Why do blokes ignore their physical health, knowing the mental and emotional toll? Denial. We think, *I'll sort it next week, my body's got this covered. A few quiet drinks won't hurt, and I'll rest during my holidays next month.* Excuses keep piling up. Meanwhile, my internal dialogue was trying to warn them, *Mate, how do you think those 10 schooners of beer twice a week, along with Maccas for lunch, are affecting you?*

But it's easier to judge other people than to deal with our own health, and a troubling aspect of this lack of self-awareness is the judgement of others' physical appearance as they age, especially women. "Geez, she's carrying a bit of timber, what's going on there?"

Susan: Obviously something changed, Matt. You take really good care of yourself now. What happened?

Matt: I got asked a simple question at just the right time: "How do you want to impact your kids' lives and interact with your grandkids?"

I gave a pretty predictable response, but my mentor followed up with, "So what are you doing with what you already know to make that happen?"

My initial answer was a lie: "I've got a plan and will start at the end of the month."

His response was the wake-up call: "Matt, you can waste all the time you like, but be aware you can't buy it." I had to sit with that and understand what he meant. Then it hit me: the time I waste can't be given back. Life doesn't offer refunds. Use it or lose it. This realisation changed my approach that very day. Maybe this is one of the reasons I love questions so much. When they land at just the right time, it can change everything.

So, Susan, what keeps you motivated to stay physically active in the second half?

Susan: The first moment of realisation came quite a while ago. I was in my kitchen and could hear shrieks of excitement and fits of laughter coming from my boy, who was 8 at the time. I looked out, wondering what was going on. To my astonishment, I saw him playing a game of rugby ... with my 70-something-year-old mother! She was running the length of the yard, ready for a touchdown, and he was in hot pursuit. It made me smile, and I felt a mix of gratitude and admiration. Nearly 10 years later, she's still the coolest nanny I know, and my kids are so lucky to have her.

For me, physical health is about the currency of energy. Put simply, if you arrive at the second half of your life and your tank is empty, it needs fuel before embarking any further. I want to be like my mother. I want to create enough energy so I can do my job into my 80s. And I can't wait to play with my future grandkids, to travel everywhere in the world, and to swim in the ocean every day while I'm still on this planet.

Matt: Your Mum is really inspiring. We don't get a great deal of good news about our physical capacities pushing through halftime and moving into the second half. Chronic habits and behaviours from our early years, like excessive partying and eating poorly, start to impact. Our hormonal levels dip, often leaving us fatigued.

Then we get countless pieces of conflicting and evolving advice from so-called ageing experts; everything from using pharmaceuticals through to standing barefooted on the grass. I definitely don't want to add to the complexity by spewing endless scientific studies all over you. Yes, I've got a tertiary qualification in Sports Science, but I've learnt just as much from playing and coaching in professional elite sports for well over 30-years, and overcoming my own autoimmune disease.

In the pursuit of a thriving second half, I asked myself: *What do you want your later decades to look like, and what's your plan for the rest of your life?* My goal is to be a healthy, fit 60-year-old at 80, enhancing not just life expectancy but the quality of my life. I have a deep curiosity to learn not just how to live, but how to have a fun life. That's why I'm so dedicated to giving people access to tools and approaches that actually provide the energy to enjoy themselves.

Susan: As you say, Matt, there's so much advice out there and much of it is contradictory. One day you read that chocolate is bad for you, and the next day it's a super food. A few years ago, it was all the rage to do bootcamp workouts in the park, and now it's all about lifting weights at the gym. I know you spend a lot of time guiding people through this maze. What do you tell them?

If you don't make time for your wellness, you'll be forced to take time for your illness.

Joyce Sunada, wellness educator

Matt: It's worth just percolating on that quote for a moment. What we share here isn't rocket science, but many of us brush it off because of its simplicity. Trust me, the moment something is complex, it is probably not serving you.

People hear me say this a lot: *"It's not what you know, it's what you do with your knowledge that turns it into wisdom"*.

Everyone knows not to smoke, right? But still, many make the choice to go down that path. Wisdom is about using your understanding and instincts to serve your own wellbeing.

When looking at physical health, the usual topics of exercise, diet, breathing and sleep will come up. Let's debunk the complexity and get to the heart of the matter. The most crucial factor is cultivating healthy lifestyle routines that support your wellbeing. Whether it's breathing, sleeping, exercising or eating, these elements are interconnected. Breathe better, relax more, sleep soundly, make better food choices, energise yourself to exercise, and watch the cycle unfold. We're not reinventing the wheel, we're optimising it.

Susan: Everything you says applies equally to women. That being said, masculine energy is different to feminine energy.

Take the title of this book for example. When you shared your idea for 'winning the second half', I felt a small wave of exhaustion. I've spent a lifetime winning at my career, raising kids and establishing my life, and the last thing I was up for was more winning. Playing, yes! Playing the second half I was down for. Thriving in the second half, definitely! Sleeping through the second half was also a distinct possibility. I have years of that to catch up on.

Our chats often reveal the fundamental differences between masculine and feminine energy. Masculine energy is designed to do, drive, win, achieve. Feminine energy is more receptive and designed to flow, create and play.

Matt: But Susan, you're one of the best people I know for driving something to an outcome and getting things done! How do you explain that?

"It's not what you know, it's what you do with your knowledge that turns it into wisdom".

Susan: I'm not saying women can't bring masculine energy to things. Sometimes we're even better at it than men. And I certainly know men who can tap into their feminine energy better than some of my female friends. But I can tell you that when masculine energy dominated my life, I achieved lots of goals but felt empty inside. In fact, it led to my quarter life crisis where I questioned the value of ticking off a to-do list.

I learnt that I can dip in and out of the parts of life that demand me to do, achieve, drive and win; lots of my corporate work is defined by this sort of need. But I know when it's time for me to switch it off and let my natural, feminine spirit take the lead.

It's helpful to look at energy as a commodity, a very valuable one. Think about the last time you had overflowing energy and your cup was full. Chances are you were in a great mood, could see things with greater clarity, and were able to tackle challenges that might have previously seemed insurmountable. These are all the qualities you need to live a fulfilled life. The more energy you have, the more you can take on the world. But how full is your energy cup right now after the last few busy decades? 10%? 50%?

Before you consider the 'what next?' of the second half, it's important to get that cup full to overflowing. Having dreams, goals and opportunities is one thing, but you've then got to ask yourself: *What energy do I need to live the second half I truly desire?*

We often pay more attention to the energy we use: the output. It's more visible and obvious: "I'm exhausted from that busy day." "Menopause is sucking the life out of me." "My body is tired from our hike this morning." "My mind is fried from learning new things all day." We often don't consider the input of energy – the fuel we need to meet the demands of our lives. I believe we should dedicate time every single day to cultivating the energy we need for our life.

The best sources of energy come from how we use our body, and how we feed and nurture her (or him). I agree with you, Matt, that the main and most powerful ways we boost our energy are through exercise and movement, nutrition, rest and one of our most undiscovered but potent resources, our breath.

Matt: Susan, I'm really keen to see how your insights on these differences play out in these tips and recommendations. I think a lot of them suit both men and women, but I'm guessing you will push me a bit further in my thinking, and probably in the way I practise my own second-half rituals and routines.

I explain it all through what I call the DESIRgram (Diet Exercise Sleep Inspiring Recovery).

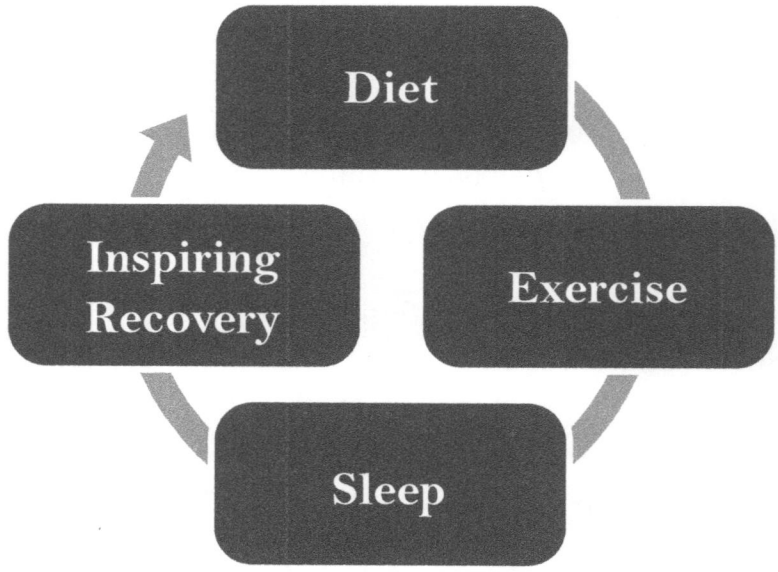

Susan: Let's do it, Matt.

Chapter 18

Diet

Matt: First, let me say I'm not a big fan of the word 'diet', as it speaks to so many people in the context of losing weight and focusing on what you can't eat. I'd rather focus on what you can eat, and how best to shape that into your life to elevate your health and make meal time something to enjoy.

Susan: You're certainly speaking to women, when you highlight how loaded the word 'diet' is. If you're a woman in midlife, chances are, like me, you have partaken in a few dieting fads: The Hip and Thigh Diet, The Atkins Diet, the Zone Diet. The diet merry-go-round is often responsible for slowing and confusing your metabolism.

Matt: I mentioned earlier that I have an autoimmune disease, and I understand the consequences of not following very simple protocols. After great medical support, I was told I would need to take a steroid for the rest of my life. Fortunately, I met Anthony Minichiello around the same time and he introduced me to the Weston A Price approach to eating. Within 6 weeks, I was off all medication.

After having no symptoms for 13 years and then failing to observe the protocols, I woke up just after Christmas suffering acute pain in all my joints. It even hurt to touch my skin. While I recognised the symptoms, I thought I'd caught influenza from my grandson, because I hadn't been ill for a long time. Literally 3 weeks later, after still eating poorly, overexercising and attending a stressful family event, the symptoms returned with a vengeance. It was like someone shouting, "If you don't want to pay attention, we'll make the consequences worse!"

Following are my 8 simple tips on how you can improve your health and vitality through healthy eating. I understand that everyone reading this won't have the same challenges, but the principles shared here will build your personal energy, deliver mental clarity, and make you feel balanced emotionally.

Tip 1: Share Meals with Loved Ones

The 'Blue Zones', 6 areas around the planet that have the highest concentration of people over 100 years of age, showed that while these people had healthy diets and did incidental exercise, the biggest common denominator was that the majority of time they had meals promoting human interaction, which feeds the prime human need of safety.

We are genetically designed to sit down with people we trust in a safe environment. Back when we lived in caves, if we were around people we trusted, we were likely to get food. If we were on our own or around people we didn't trust, we were likely to become food! While we have evolved in so many ways, this is still a part of our DNA. So, if you've got the healthiest plate of food in front of you but are stressed, angry or anxious, you may as well not eat. Your fight or flight system will be activated, with your sympathetic nervous system signalling your body not to use energy on digestion, because the shit is about to hit the fan. Coupled with this, stress hormones, like adrenaline and cortisol, suppress the function of the digestive system. Sitting down with those you love, good friends or a great work colleague will not only make the meal more enjoyable, you'll also eat a touch slower because you are in conversation, and you'll be activating the hormones of wellbeing like serotonin and oxytocin, which elevate your digestive system.

This may not be possible at every meal for a variety of reasons, but try to schedule it at least once every 2 days.

Tip 2: Eat Food with One Ingredient

How many ingredients are there in an apple or a steak or a zucchini? It's not a trick question – yes, you got it right if you said 'one'. The more we consume whole foods, the more we access the nutrients they have on offer.

Eat fruit and veggies that haven't been exposed to insecticides, or clean your fruit and veggies by soaking them in baking soda and apple cider vinegar, then rinsing them off.

This reduces potential inflammatory impacts of chemicals.

Know how your protein has been reared, for example, cows and salmon don't eat grain naturally, so it makes sense that feeding them grains doesn't make them healthy. For example, eating grain-fed beef creates an imbalance in your Omega 6 and Omega 3 ratio, resulting in inflammatory impacts for those who consistently eat this product. It's difficult to derive health out of an unhealthy animal.

Tip 3: Eat as Little as Possible from a Packet

This is my trick way of saying limit the amount of processed food you eat. Many ingredients used in these foods include sugar, soy, vegetable oils, emulsifiers and processed starch. All of these have been proven to compromise health, by causing inflammation, fat gain and digestive disorders. In modern life, it's difficult to abide by this 100 percent of the time, but if you can observe this protocol most of the time, I assure you the results will be quickly evident.

Tip 4: Get Veggies to Occupy More of Your Plate

Here in Australia, when we have a steak there is often very little space to fit anything else on the plate. I suggest that you reverse this, and let vegetables dominate your plate, with your protein being about the size of the palm of your hand.

Tip 5: Eat Less Often, not Less

Giving your digestive system a rest for at least 12 hours every day does a few things: resets your gut, reduces blood sugar levels and, after 16 hours, human growth hormone levels increase and you start burning fat, which is our cleanest source of energy.

Let me put some better context behind this:

If you have dinner at 7pm and breakfast at 7am you've reduced your blood sugar. If you can stretch that out to 11am, you will boost human growth hormone and start fat burning. On the odd occasion you get to 1pm, a process called autophagy kicks in. Your body starts feeding on itself, beginning with the breakdown of old cells. This allows your cellular function to operate at a higher level and decreases inflammation in the body.

Remember, this tip encourages you to eat less often, rather than less food.

Tip 6: Multivitamin Supplement

The way most modern food is raised, whether it be a plant or a beast, the concentration of vitamins and minerals available in our soil is much lower than it used to be. I could go on about how Big Ag is consistently turning soil into dirt, but how about we leave that to the next book. The key point to share is that we don't get these crucial elements we need to support our health from most food. I would suggest a high-quality supplement that recognises your gender and any health challenges you have, and don't forget to include an Omega 3 supplement.

Tip 7: What to Limit

At the risk of being slightly repetitious, I want to reinforce the things you should try to minimise in your eating plan:

- *sugar*
- *alcohol*
- *starch and gluten*
- *processed foods*

Tip 8: What to Eat More Of

Eat more:

- *quality plant-based food*
- *quality fats from healthy animals or avocados*
- *quality sourced protein*

> *Become aware of your body's response to all foods. For most people, the 80/20 rule works, which means they can eat healthily 80% of the time, and occasionally cheat with a chocolate ice-cream or Macca's burger. Recently, I've learnt that rule doesn't apply to me; my body sent me severe consequences to show me loud and clear that there are some foods I can never eat.*

Susan: I gave up diet fads many years ago, but like you, Matt, I've also got an autoimmune condition in Hashimoto's disease and type 1 diabetes, which I've had since I was 17 years old. It makes me pay a lot of attention to how my body reacts to all sorts of foods, and it tells me really fast when I'm off track.

But when you're young, you don't want to miss out on anything; it took me until around 40 before I finally had a pretty good idea of what worked for me, and before I had the motivation to stick with it. Many people I know say they feel good when they follow a similar regime, even if they don't have a medical condition.

This is what I did for me. I created a list of diet rules which I'll now share with you:

Susan's Top 8 Diet Rules

1. Remove gluten.
2. Limit dairy.
3. Focus on protein rich food – I aim to get 30g of protein in at every meal. This helps protect against the loss of lean muscle mass.
4. Make most of your plate vegetables and salad. I use carbohydrates as a carrier of the main event – protein and nutrient-dense food – rather than making it the meal itself.
5. Bone broth and other healing food full of collagen are great for your skin, and are cheaper and safer than botox.
6. Prioritise foods that are rich in nutrients, with a focus on Vitamin D, K, calcium, magnesium, Omega 3s. Supplement if you're missing any of these.
7. Limit alcohol – I can be a bit hit and miss with this one, but I know that for me and many female friends, alcohol and hot flushes have a close relationship. Plus, good sleep and wine don't necessarily mix. Sugar can also play havoc with menopause symptoms.
8. Hydration is key. Hot flushes and the balancing required in the body during midlife is hugely dehydrating. Water for your cells is a priority.

I am also a believer in shaking up your diet at least every decade, so your body doesn't get 'stuck' and you don't get too rigid with your rules.

> A word on intermittent and other forms of fasting. Just like exercise, we need to approach our nutrition and eating routines by listening to our bodies as the first source of wisdom. For some women, fasting can improve menopause symptoms; for others, it can exacerbate them. Some women have found fluctuating hormones become worse, additional symptoms appear, bone density issues arise, and adrenal fatigue becomes a risk. It's up to you to listen to your body and then work with your health practitioners to decide which camp you lie in, then act accordingly.

Matt: Great reminder, Susan. We must all listen to our bodies and observe what works for us and what doesn't. The body gives us many signals, if we listen. Eating is a lot more than an equation of energy in = energy out. Food is not just fuel; our meals are something to relish, from the amazing flavours through to enjoying the company of good people.

Chapter 19

Exercise

Matt: Exercise has been a lifelong area of curiosity and where I've focused my academic pursuits. All the information shared here is genuinely relevant and can play a major part in you not only living longer but, more importantly, being healthier. Many experts argue that exercise is the most potent longevity drug. It not only delays death, but also prevents cognitive and physical decline more effectively than any other intervention. Just 3 hours of exercise per week can decrease negative biomarkers by 30 to 40 percent.

There are a couple of important things to consider about exercise and how to frame it. Firstly, exercise isn't a form of punishment or sacrifice that you must endure. As humans, we are designed to move then rest up, but the programming we get in modern life is to relentlessly pursue comfort. Our environment offers too many ways to avoid moving our bodies: take the lift rather than the stairs, get food delivered rather than walking through the supermarket, stream the world onto our TV screens rather than going out dancing.

Susan: You talked earlier about men often being in denial about their health, but we all have our avoidance strategies. *I'm starting Monday* was always a popular mantra among my friends, when we talked about getting to the gym. It's a great excuse to deal with rapidly declining willpower towards the end of the week, and we didn't want to miss the Friday night drinks with great food.

Matt: I've seen that strategy heaps, and used it! But your body craves physical exercise, and moving your body is crucial to activate all sorts of healthy responses, such as better digestion, better sleep and better mood. When you shift your focus from mere lifespan to healthspan, it's easier to break free from the allure of immediate comfort to long-term gains.

Secondly, and at the other end of the spectrum, is the pressure to exercise beyond healthy limits. Coming out of a professional sporting career as a player and coach, my conditioning was that you need to be completely flogged to get any benefit out of exercise. This mentality has been transferred to other sectors of the health and exercise industry. While elite sport requires people to be super athletic and fit, much of it isn't really that healthy for you. I probably don't need to go into detail as to why rugby league isn't that healthy for those who play it. Equally, we aren't designed to run marathons, have hard cricket balls fired towards us at 100 miles an hour while standing in the sun for 5 days, and the injury toll on knees would suggest that netball carries a lot of health risks as well.

My point is that, being healthy is not about being an elite athlete, it's about moving your body in ways that promote growth and restoration. We must all find the right balance to suit our goals and our lifestyle.

Susan: I agree with that statement completely, Matt. I have a lot of female friends who run marathons, do triathlons, long-distance ocean swims, hiking and mountain runs, so I am not saying that women aren't competitive and driven or can't be serious sportspeople. No way! I simply invite all women (and men too, if they are willing to give it a go) to discover other ways of moving that support feminine energy. If anyone is still wondering what I mean about masculine energy and feminine energy, let me tell you about a scene I see often.

I'm in love with the sunrise, especially when I'm walking along a rugged coastline that hugs the clear blue sea full of its magical creatures. I love the way the trees bend together over my walking path, as if to form a guard of honour welcoming me to its majestic wonderland. I regularly hike 7km in Noosa National Park and my body feels so connected to everything around me. Every 15 metres, I see a frame of something gorgeous, better than any gallery art. That early in the morning, the only people I pass are men, and lots of them. And they're not very friendly. My smiles and soft 'good mornings' are met with … well, nothing. Their eyes tend to be fixed, minds focused, bodies engaged. I see the cliffs as something to love, admire and breathe in. They see them as mountains to conquer. My fellow sisters are the smart ones, just surfacing from their beds on my return an hour later.

This experience has really brought home to me that masculine and feminine energy are different. Masculine energy is penetrative. It is designed to drive, achieve, compete and … conquer! While feminine energy can be slow to get started, it builds like a waterfall, gathers momentum and flows like a stream. It's designed to be receptive, sensual, creative, joyful. It winds and bends, ebbs and flows.

Matt: I think what you are talking about is the 'joy of movement'. Everyone needs to find something they love, so exercise is no longer a chore. My approach is to break down exercise into 4 crucial components: strength, stability, aerobic efficiency and VO2 max. Susan, I think we should add another one: energy. While your tips do fit into the other 4 components, I recognise you're going to make us think deeply about how to work with our own energy.

Before we dive in, the tips below are what I have incorporated in my life, but I strongly advise everyone to consult your physician or exercise expert before you start, to tailor the program that aligns with your unique needs.

Strength

Strength training not only combats muscle loss by engaging in practical movement with resistance, it is also essential for daily activities and injury prevention. Loading your body with a greater level of resistance than normal also spikes a hormonal response that goes beyond just muscle repair to also spike cognitive and cardiovascular function.

Now let's be clear with this, you don't need to sign up to a gym, buy tight clothes and stand in front of mirrors. This is purely about slightly and progressively overloading your body. Having said that, there are real advantages in using the right gym for 2 key reasons:

Most gyms have equipment that assists in the safe and controlled lifting of greater weight across your entire body, allowing for gradual increase of load. The micro-tears this ignites in your muscles are where the abovementioned benefits come from.

A gym offers the opportunity to interact with others, and get and give support to a training partner. This creates the opportunity to extend yourself more than you might do alone, create some accountability, and elevate the safety of your sessions. Most importantly, training with friends introduces fun into what too many people see as a burden.

Other ways I get resistance training:

I use resistance bands at home.

I go to a park gym nearby.

I put weight in a backpack and do squats, push-ups and chins. (You can go on YouTube to see the best ways to do this)

Doing this type of session 2-3 times a week for 30 minutes will have a significant impact on your health and longevity.

Stability

Stability training integrates balance practices into your daily life for mental and physical equilibrium, reducing susceptibility to injuries. Falls are the leading cause of death and hospitalisation in Australia, with the frequency increasing with age.

Key ways to develop stability through balance and core strength can be found by participating in some well-known movement practices. My choices include:

- ✓ Pilates
- ✓ Yoga

However, here are my simple, everyday key practices in this area:

- *Brushing my teeth standing on one leg with my eyes closed, using both hands and changing legs. Standing very close to the sink, I rarely get through a full cycle without putting my other leg down or grabbing the sink.*
- *Doing one-legged squats, not holding on to anything, while making my morning coffee.*

This sounds very simple and you might find it difficult to see how it can be of benefit. So, allow me to explain it in another way: my balancing practice at the sink takes 3 minutes twice a day, and my one-legged balancing squats take 4 minutes before getting in my car every morning. This total of 10 minutes of stability work is something I never miss, regardless of where I am or what I'm doing. Amounting to 70 minutes a week, it means I spend nearly 5 hours every month on my stability. So, you see, it's possible to enhance your physical capacity without a lot of impact on your schedule.

Aerobic Efficiency

I used to think of aerobic training as 10 kilometre runs, an hour on a training bike, or getting pumped on the rower. The modern and healthy interpretation of aerobic training is 30-40 minutes of moderate exercise, where you are still able to share short sentences or continue breathing through your nose. Brisk walks with a friend, a swim at the local pool, a cycle to your local café, or jumping on the elliptical machine at the gym all hit the mark. You'll be boosting life enjoyment while improving mitochondrial health, fat burning, and enhancing cardiovascular capacity through conversational aerobic fitness.

My strong suggestion is to do this in the morning, outside when possible, so you get some early morning sun in your eyes. This exposes you to some important vitamin D and also kick-starts the production of melatonin, which will help you sleep that night. If you want to go full tilt like me, have an ice bath or cold shower to increase core blood flow and stimulate your lymphatic system to enhance health and healing.

If you do your aerobic exercise consistently 5-7 times a week, it will move from being a burden to something you become attached to for personal productivity and energy throughout the day.

VO2 max

This style is quite different to 'conversational' fitness, even though it is done in similar ways, such as running, cycling or rowing. Rather than maintaining a steady pace, you are going to have short intervals where you go as hard as you can.

It has a few real key benefits, including elevation of oxygen utilisation, which is associated with increased lifespan, and hormonal spikes that improve anti-ageing by delivering testosterone and human growth hormone to our system.

One thing I feel very strongly about with this type of training is that 'high intensity' is about your measurement, not what someone else thinks you should be doing. The protocol I use once a week for 15-20 minutes is done on a stationary bike or rower, as the risk of pulling a muscle is greatly reduced compared to running. I commence with 5 minutes of gentle warm-up, then go as hard as I can for 30 seconds, then rest for one minute. I repeat this 5-7 times. Remember that your version of 'hard as you can' will be different to mine and that's the way it should be.

My strong recommendation is to do a VO2 max session once per week. It's tough, but the benefits are amazing.

Susan: Matt, you've provided some excellent tips, and your tips made me immediately change my exercise routine. I now brush my teeth balancing on one leg too!

Matt: Not always easy, is it? But I think the fun exercises are the best. Fun and human connection can be incorporated into each of the 4 key exercise protocols above. Here are some of the things I do to mix fun and human connection in with ticking off my healthy exercise practices.

At least 3 times a week at 7am, I walk with my grandson to our local café. But before I pick him up, I take a morning ice bath. An ice bath prior to exercise promotes blood flow to my brain and vital organs. This is ideal aerobic training, while building an amazing relationship with my grandson.

For nearly 15 years, I've been paddling on ocean skis with one of my best friends twice a week in the Royal National Park in Sydney. While I don't view this as exercise, we paddle for around an hour every time we go. It's not a competition to see who wins (well, it kind of is, as we continually and subconsciously test each other). Jeff is a proud First Nations man and knows many sites where Aboriginal art and caves are located. All 4 exercise protocols are touched on while doing this: our VO2 max capacities are raised when paddling side by side on the home straight, stability is elevated when we catch waves, and upper-body strength obviously increases. Most importantly, we're connecting to country with great chats. In the whole time we have been paddling, I can't remember not having fun.

Susan: These examples also have elements of feminine energy in them, Matt, which shows that men also benefit from balancing their more traditional exercise with movement that flows. When you're out paddling, do the 2 of you ever just stop and allow the movement of the water to gently rock your body? This is the movement of feminine energy. It doesn't work in rigid up and down motion, but more in cyclical flow. Imagine you have a hula hoop and you are circling it up and down your body – that's a pretty close representation. It's the feeling of dancing in the loungeroom or swimming under a waterfall, or doing cat-cow in yoga class. It is designed to circle your body and curve up your spine. Any movement you do that is circular or allows the spine to curl and bend is super nourishing.

> ### Feminine Energy
>
> *For women, tapping into our feminine energy is essential for health. Men can benefit by unlocking this energy too.*
>
> *Incorporate flowing movements, where you curl and curve your spine, into your routine. Here are some examples:*
>
> - *Swimming*
> - *Tai chi*
> - *Hula hoop*
> - *Dance*
> - *Yoga (just 3 minutes of cat-cow pose will have you feeling great!)*
> - *Slowly curling down and up while you touch your toes*

Susan: I'm definitely no athlete, but my physical fitness has been a priority since I attended daily aerobics classes in my fluoro leotard in high school in the 80s. Over this time, I have learnt about the different fitness regimes for different phases of your life and I've changed my routines often. In the second half, peri and menopause have significant impacts on a woman's body. It's working hard dealing with fluctuating hormones, shifting energy levels, interrupted sleep, as well as softening and sore joints and bones.

During menopause, I experienced more joint pain and stiffness in my elbows, knees and feet. Hormones had caused a softening that felt similar to when I was first pregnant. This meant changing my exercise. I stopped using the treadmill and took up swimming and cycling for a period of time. Now the hormonal peaks have shifted, I can cope with any exercise again.

Physical exercise can be great for menopause symptoms and certainly needs to be on the agenda for the biggest symptom that most women are concerned about: weight gain. But it is crucial to recognise that your body is already using a considerable amount of energy, and sometimes taking your foot off the pedal is required. Pay attention to how your body is feeling and adjust accordingly. For example, some women find high intensity workouts and interval training increase their hot flushes. For others, it's the key to managing their menopause symptoms. Be your own fitness coach.

> ## Listen to Your Body and Adapt
>
> *Everyone has different needs and issues when it comes to physical exercise. There is definitely no 'one size fits all'. If you listen closely, your body will tell you what you need to do when it comes to physical exercise and movement, and don't be surprised if it's different to your friends or family. It will also change at different stages of your life, so let go of the aspiration to exercise like your 18-year-old self. Pay attention to aches and pains because they are good guides. Always ask yourself:*
>
> *What does my body need?*
>
> *How is my body reacting to that?*

Susan: I'm talking to the women now, but I'm sure this is interesting for men too. One of the great things about a feminine body is she talks to you loudly. Some attribute that to intuition, and that's certainly the case when you get a message or gut feeling. But there's a scientific explanation that reveals why our body is so good at telling us when we have pushed it too hard. Here's a few interesting facts:[7]

Women are better at picking up on the signals than our male peers, because it appears pain systems differ between the genders. Studies have found that women have a more intense

---

7 - See References 7.

pain response, having twice as many pain receptors. The jury is out on whether that is due to our greater nerve density or whether hormones are at play. We know that women's experience of pain is different to men's. (Hello, man flu!) Our pain threshold may be greater for evolutionary reasons, making it even more important to listen to your body's signals and cues.

- **Women have fewer pain blockers then men.** *Research has revealed it takes twice as much morphine to ease pain for females than for males. Apparently, we don't have as many mu opioid receptors. Never heard of them? I hadn't either, but their role is to bring in the feel-good endorphins that reduce pain.*
- **Hormones really do make a difference.** *Women have lower levels of testosterone, which influences the experience of pain. The higher the testosterone, the more you are protected from the feeling of pain.*

Why am I telling you this? Because we have very sophisticated systems for detecting when something is 'off'. But the question is, are we using that?

A few other things I now include for my exercise in the second half may be useful for other women. Interesting Matt that we are both drawn to the cold experience!

Exercise for Women in the Second Half

It's really important around menopause to do something that makes you sweat and puff every single day. Get your heart rate up! Ten minutes is what I aim for every day somewhere in my workout hour, then I move on to other forms of exercise.

Strength training is so important for our muscles and bones so, Matt, your tips are highly relevant. We lose muscle faster post-menopause. I hit the gym for weight training 3 times a week. Having your own hand weights is also a great help!

Cold showers are my drug of choice. Every morning, whether it's -6°C or 36°C, I jump straight into the shower, spine first, before turning around and putting my face up to the water. It invigorates every cell. I do an occasional ice bath, but showers are something I can do daily and they really make a difference to balancing my body and mind.

Research suggests you should take this to the pool or ocean if you can. A recent study[8] found that menopausal women who regularly swim in cold water report significant improvements to their physical and mental health. The research found that menopausal women experienced a significant improvement in anxiety (46.9 percent), mood swings (34.5 percent), low mood (31.1 percent) and hot flushes (30.3 percent), as a result of cold-water swimming. Now if that's not a reason

---

8 - See References 8.

to push yourself out of your comfort zone, then I'm not sure what is!

On a final note, don't forget your pelvic floor muscles, which weaken as you age. This doesn't have to be complicated. Sitting at your computer, you can do 3 sets of 15 squeezes of your pelvic floor and it will make a difference (and give you a little more confidence when exercising too!).

Chapter 20

Sleep to Thrive

Matt: We've all had a shit night's sleep and experienced tiredness, lack of focus and crankiness, so most of us understand the importance of sleep for our health. The cumulative impacts of not sleeping well, or resting up when needed, stack up very poorly against the topic of this book, winning the second half of life. Having an understanding what goes on in slumber, and how to create a routine that elevates the wellbeing benefits, is important.

Susan: I know it's not a competition but a shit night's sleep doesn't even come close to describing what many women experience in menopause. This is a big one for women for many reasons. When I reached 50, I realised I was exhausted, not from the week, month or year, but from the last 30 years. There was no gap year for me, no sabbatical or change of pace. Downtime was treated as time to fill with more activities. When I took maternity leave, I launched a new arm of my business, wrote a book and renovated our house at the same time! I don't think I'd be alone here.

The feminine body isn't designed for excessive doing. As we discussed earlier, it is receptive in nature, unlike masculine energy which is designed for doing, achieving and pursuing.

The reality is we'll burn out quicker and we need more rest than men.

The wisdom central to our Wise Woman phase won't arise out of busyness. If you stay in busy and fast energy, you'll not only end up exhausted, you will be less likely to fully embrace the magic of this phase. With so many people entering their second half still only part way through building careers, raising families, accruing wealth and creating stability, there's a huge risk that their bodies are not being nurtured with enough rest for healthy ageing.

Matt: That's what I see again and again. I don't want to dive too deep into the science of sleep, not only because I could bore the shit out of you, but because I don't want to scare you off. So, allow me to start this with a very common-sense approach to sleep.

When we sleep, a lot of our key bodily functions get the opportunity to gear down. One of the biggest users of energy, our digestive tract, turns off. Our biggest mental stimulator, vision, is switched off. The need to move our largest muscle groups is massively decreased. Our decision-making leader, our brain, can shut down cognitive operations. As a result of this massive reduction of activity in our body, the opportunity arises to send our 'cleaners' in to accelerate healing, restore energy and prepare the removal of toxins from our body.

Modern life has reduced our sleep time, because of our ability to turn lights on at night and be stimulated by televisions, laptops and phones. Those cleaners who are waiting for the night shift to do their good work throughout our body have less time to get the job done with the same equipment.

We have 3 levels of sleep:

1. Light Sleep
2. Deep Sleep and
3. Rapid Eye Movement (REM)

All are very important to support functional life. The one that's most compromised by evening stimulation is deep sleep, which then affects our REM (dreaming state). So, let's explore what the answer is to this challenge.

The following principles and routines will improve the quality of your sleep, prioritising restoration and building energy.

Sleep Routine

This is essential to improve your sleep hygiene. Most functional things in life are closely linked to habits, and quality sleep definitely falls into this category. Now, we all understand it is not possible to adhere to routines 100 percent of the time, as life tends to drag us away from this for either good or bad reasons. However, being able to stick to a solid routine as much as possible has positive impacts on longevity and vibrancy.

Target a 7 to 8-hour sleeping window, and slot it into regular times. For example, get into bed between 9 to 10.30pm, with your wake-up time between 5 to 6.30am. This sleeping window is certainly adaptable around personal preferences and work times, but it is important to recognise that our genetic circadian rhythm is impacted by the sun. Build the following protocols into this routine:

- *10 hours before sleep, no more coffee*
- *3 hours before sleep, have your last meal and alcoholic drink*
- *2 hours before sleep, turn as many lights off in your house as possible*
- *1 hour before sleep, turn off all devices and TV*

Get Morning Sunshine

Getting 10 minutes of direct sunlight before 10am (even if it's overcast) will stop the production of your sleep hormone melatonin, allowing it to have a more positive impact on your sleep pattern that evening.

Dark Room

Making your room as dark as possible helps the body to continue the production of melatonin. Even exposure to small amounts of light can suppress this and negatively impact your sleep.

Cool Room

The ideal sleep temperature is around 18°C, allowing our body temperature to drop and elevate our ability to enter deep sleep. This doesn't mean you have lie on top of the sheets and shiver; just exposing your face and hands supports this important process.

Reduce Noise

While this is obvious, many choose to just suck it up and do their best. If you live in a noisy area, I strongly suggest you buy yourself a good set of comfortable earplugs, as you could get all the other protocols in perfect order, but they can be gazumped by this.

Breath Work, Meditation or Mindfulness to Unwind

These practices will show up in other sections of this book, as both Susan and I are massive advocates. However, across all cultures, elite athletes and intellects, relaxing our bodies through deep nasal breathing, while narrowing our focus to a single point of attention, signals our brain that it's time switch the body off and prepare for sleep. While there are a few different methods to do this, here are a few suggestions: Kelee Meditation App, Take A Breath, 478 Mindfulness Breathing, or Dr Joe Dispenza Evening Sleep Meditation on YouTube.

Sound Down to Wind Down

When explaining this to groups, I often start by using my loud coach whistle, which is extremely high-pitched. Not only does this surprise people, it puts the audience in a very alert mode. Their brains go into high Beta wave mode, signalling the body to be ready for action. This is exactly what happens when we hear a loud noise that surprises us and makes us jump. So, it's got to make sense that, if certain noise can heighten alertness, other types of noise can signal

> *our brain that we are safe and ready to relax. This can be achieved by listening to Theta wave music, which has the opposite effect to the fight, flight or freeze response, allowing the brain and body to relax and switch off. Search for Theta wave sleep music on YouTube, to find the reel that suits you best.*

Matt: Recently, after having my knee replaced due to past sporting injuries, even with all my sleep protocols in place, I still struggled to get a decent night's sleep until introducing Theta wave music into my routine. I haven't needed this music since completing my recovery, however on the very odd occasion when I need to let go of the stress of the day, this is definitely a go-to that works every time.

Susan: Great tips, Matt. I've polished up my sleep routine after hearing this. I would also encourage people to bring more rest into their waking hours. As we age, those long hours of being switched on seem to be more tiring. Plus for women, all the sleep strategies in the world won't necessarily fix the menopausal sleep interruptions. Some nights I would be waking every hour and had to employ techniques similar to having a newborn. I would have micro-naps during the day and generally needed to pull back my energy.

A decade ago, when I felt out of balance and depleted, I rearranged my work schedule to include more breaks. Previously, I was like most people scheduling a big 'once a year' holiday, but not giving much consideration to the downtime needed in the remaining part of the year.

Reflecting on the feminine cyclic nature, I came up with the idea of having 'seasons' of work, with breaks in between to replenish. Every quarter, I would take a short break and a longer break at the end of the year. This is when I learnt the beauty of space and rest. During these breaks, I would spend time in nature with my tribe. I would enjoy long walks and swims in the ocean. There was no timetable or schedule. I did what my body desired. These breaks led to the next season being more creative, productive and fulfilling. I did my best work after my seasonal breaks; opportunities came flooding in when I opened that space.

There are many ways for people to honour rest. It might be my European heritage, but I'm all for bringing back the after-lunch siesta! However, rest doesn't need to be sleep. Some people may just need time away from others to be in solitude for a while. Others might benefit from reduced 'productive' hours to spend more time in a flow state. The process of discovery will teach you a lot about who you are and what you need in your second half.

Chapter 21

Breathing for Life

Matt: In our daily lives, we take approximately 22,000 breaths without much conscious thought. The simplicity of this act may deceive us into overlooking its profound importance. Yet, a mere pause in breathing for a minute will underscore its critical role in signalling our wellbeing. Exploring the transformative power of intentional breathing practices reveals how they can positively impact mental, physical and emotional health.

Susan: Breathwork ... hell, yes! Life-changing. Every moment is an opportunity to slow down and connect with your breathing. We women can be notoriously bad at stopping, which means we're very rarely resting and replenishing. How many times have you sat down on the couch, only to be bombarded with all the things you should be doing?

If you feel like you've been racing through half your life, chances are you have been moving fast and breathing shallow. This is not a good place to be and, as you age, your body will have less tolerance for it. Every practice I do now, whether it's physical, mental, spiritual or emotional, has a foundation of breath work.

At the very least ... 2 periods of 11 minutes a day, consciously breathing (feel your breath move in and out of your body) and relaxing will change your midlife!

What tips do you have, Matt?

Matt: Back in 2014, at the suggestion of my friend and World Surfing Champ Mick Fanning, I delved into the world of performance breathing, under the guidance of Nam Baldwin. At the time, this practice was unconventional, but its efficacy in enhancing performance and wellbeing has since been well accepted.

Before delving into specific breathing techniques, it's crucial to emphasise the concept of 'practice'. Similar to exercise, reaping the benefits of breathing practices requires consistency, understanding the purpose, and a systematic approach with adequate rest.

Morning Ritual: The Wim Hof Method

Start your day with the Wim Hof Method, involving 30-40 rapid deep mouth breaths, followed by exhaling and holding your breath for as long as possible. Repeat this cycle 3 times, incorporating 20 nasal pumps for each nostril in the middle of each round. Research supports the immune system stimulation, increased energy, focus and reduced stress associated with this method.

Pre-Exercise Breathing: Block Breathing

Prior to exercise or during warm-up, engage in block breathing to signal your brain that you are in control and ready. Inhale for 4 seconds, hold for 4 seconds, exhale slowly for 4 seconds, and hold again for 4 seconds. Repeat the cycle 4 to 5 times, fostering a sense of preparedness and energy utilisation.

In-Performance Nasal Breathing

Amid exercise or challenging situations, employ nasal breathing. Inhale slowly, directing your focus to the breath's journey through your nostrils and down the back of your throat. On the exhale, shift attention externally, relaxing your jaw, face and shoulders. Repeat 2 to 3 times, enhancing focus and presence in the moment.

Post-Performance Recovery

After physically, mentally or emotionally demanding activities, wind down your nervous system for optimal health and functionality. Lie down, close your eyes, and engage in slow, smooth nasal breathing into your diaphragm. On exhales, focus on relaxing specific body regions in cycles, promoting deep relaxation and recovery. This normally takes me under 10 minutes ... unless I fall asleep, which sometimes happens.

Breathing to Reduce Anxiety

A recent addition involves a deep breath in through the nose, followed by another short breath in through the nose. Then a deep sigh through the mouth. Repeated 2 to 3 times, this technique, shared by Dr Andrew Huberman of Stanford University, signals your autonomic nervous system to relax, proving effective in high-stress situations.

Matt: Through these intentional breathing practices, I have experienced enhanced mental clarity, sustained physical energy, improved resilience and a fortified immune system. As you journey through the various methods, remember that the true power lies not just in the act of breathing, but in the intentional and consistent practice of it.

Chapter 22

Final Words

You are potentially sitting on the cusp of the most exciting, powerful phase of your life, but are you ready for it? Are you refreshed? Is your energy cup overflowing? Do you have fuel in the tank for the rest of the journey? And have you stopped to acknowledge all of the wonderful, impactful things you achieved in your first half?

As you change seasons in the trajectory of your life, it's the moments in between that hold most power. Sitting at the crossroads, you have 2 choices:

1. You can race into the second half with depleted energy and outdated routines, missing the opportunity to find a new way to thrive. This path is likely to lead to burnout, stress and ill health; or

2. You can take the opportunity to properly rest, move your body how it wants to be moved, nourish yourself, and breathe into a fresh phase. This path can enhance your healthspan and lead to the best years yet!

Not only will you derive the benefits we've discussed in this section, but recently validated science shows that your muscles are like endocrine organs. When you contract them, dopamine and serotonin move into your body. The scientist called these 'Hope Molecules'; they not only improved fitness, but also brain health, mood regulation, anxiety and depression. The way to access this internal pharmacy is simply to contract your muscles: exercise, dance, walk, swim, ride a bike or have fun playing with your family.

You are potentially sitting on the cusp of the most exciting, powerful phase of your life.

Section 5
Happy and Healthy Mind

Chapter 23

Midlife Mind Motivation

Susan's written 4 books on this topic, and I was looking forward to diving in. But first, she had a question for me.

Susan: What's going on in a man's brain, Matt? I'm constantly amazed how men can compartmentalise things, zeroing in on something and blocking everything else out. Do you feel like our brains are totally different? It seems to be more noticeable as we age!

Matt: I definitely don't think about the same things as my female friends. I admire their ability to stay across a million issues and multitask, but I've heard that men's brains are 10 percent larger. Does that mean we have superior brain power?

Susan: No, and before you get too cocky, Matt, it has nothing to do with intelligence. The inferior-parietal lobule tends to be larger in males. This part of the brain is associated with mathematical problems, estimating time and judging speed. The men in my life are definitely better at those things than I am, but I also know women who are good at them too. Like all things, the science can only tell us things in general. Individuals vary a lot. But it's still worth knowing some of the interesting differences that scientists have discovered between the male and female brain. Do you want to hear them?[9]

---
9 - See References 9.

Matt: Anything that helps me understand women better is great. Bring it on.

Susan: Female brains are more interconnected between the left and right hemispheres, while the connections in male brains are stronger between the front and back regions. This may explain why women seem to be strong in intuitive thinking, analysing and drawing conclusions. Men, on the other hand, seem to have heightened perception and stronger motor skills.

Matt: Is that why women so quickly get to conclusions I can't even see? I just can't win an argument!

Susan: Maybe. And you know how our brains have both grey and white matter? Well, there is evidence to suggest that women have more grey matter in their brains. This is where the processing of speech, sensation, perception and learning takes place. Even so, women have been found to use more of the communication capabilities of white matter, connecting processing centres, while men use more grey matter. This might explain why men tend to be great at task-focused projects, while women excel at language.

Brain ageing is also different for males and females. We all experience brain shrinkage with age, but changes appear to happen faster to the male brain. According to a 2019 study[10], the average male brain is about 3 years older, in functional terms, than the average female brain. It seems to be the opposite early in life, when young women seem to mature faster than young men.

Matt: Yes, I was one of those young men. Maybe it explains why I kept playing sport, while my sister got on with a real

---

10 - See References 10.

career! But we're talking about midlife now, and I've definitely had my senior moments recently. Cognitive decline seems to be a real thing as you get older. Have you experienced that?

Susan: Yes, brain fogginess and forgetfulness are common symptoms of menopause, but I also think this is one of the many areas women and men can relate to having the same experiences. I had one not so long ago. I left an office building after attending a day of meetings with a regular client. As I stepped onto the pavement, I ran into a participant of one of my training programs. We stopped for a nice chat, and then she asked, "Were you in here doing more of your workshops?" I started to respond, "No, I was just having a meeting with … umm … umm," and I went blank.

For the life of me, I could not recall what I was doing just 15 minutes before. I quickly wrapped it up with, "Doesn't matter, see you later!" and dashed away. I was horrified. Over the last few decades, I've secured a reputation as an expert in cultivating the mind; I've even written 4 books about it! And here I was, an absent-minded mess. Of course, the commentary part of my mind was working just fine: *Have I got early dementia? Is this what my brain is going to be like now, post-menopause? Have I scrolled too much on my phone and lost the skill of being present? Am I losing it?*

That's the day I had a good look at where I'd become complacent in my mind care. I immediately reactivated the strategies that had always worked for me, and they've definitely made a positive difference.

Matt: My brain has been on my mind too. Nothing seems to dictate your experience of ageing more than the functioning and condition of your brain. Senior moments seem to be affecting us earlier and earlier. Putting a conscious effort into cultivating a healthy and happy mind is critical at all stages of life, but once you hit midlife, you really can't ignore it anymore.

Susan: I couldn't agree more. Here's a few compelling reasons why I'm motivated to prioritise caring for my mind:

1. You are what you think.
2. Ageing affects the brain.
3. Older people can get stuck in their ruts.

You are what you think

You hear this statement all the time, but there's no place quite like middle age to see evidence of your physical body reflecting your mental state. A school reunion is the perfect stage on which to see it play out. A bunch of people who fitted neatly into the same stereotype of an age group for so long, can hit their 40s and 50s and suddenly seem generations apart. It's a shock to come together and observe that your friends could potentially be separated by a decade or more.

Take Female A for example. She had just competed in her first triathlon at 49 years of age and was enthusiastically sharing all the latest trends from the speakers at the TEDx conference she recently attended. She was full of energy, and later she was the first on the dance floor. "I still feel like I'm 17!" she exclaimed, and the truth is, she still looked and acted the same.

On the other hand, Female B sat in the corner, her body aching from standing for too long. She spoke about all the problems with the government, her frustrations with her husband and her long list of health complaints, as she drowned her sorrows with a bottle of wine. "Don't you think you're too old to wear that!" she joked with Female A. "Leave the dancing to the young ones."

Matt: I'm betting those 2 people had different sets of genetics and life experiences, but it sounds like they also had very different attitudes towards life and ageing. It reflects in their mind **and** body. The mind-body connection is well-researched, and your longevity can be impacted significantly by the way you think. We already saw in Chapter 1 that a healthy and positive mindset towards ageing literally lengthens your lifespan by more than 7 years. But it's also the determining factor in whether you will enjoy your future years, or simply tolerate them.

Ageing affects the brain

Susan: Have you noticed that you've succumbed to habits for which you previously laughed at your parents – things like calling your child by the dog's name, or having to run through all the names of people in your family before landing on the right one? Maybe you've been caught out looking for your phone, then realised you were talking on it.

Matt: Yep, many people report being slower to find words and names as they hit middle age and beyond. Other common complaints include memory loss, of course, but also struggling to focus or multitask as well as they could when they were younger.

Susan: Some of this is due to atrophy, or the 'use it or lose it' principle, which definitely applies to your neurons as much as to your muscles. But the reality is, there are also physical changes that happen in the brain as you age:

- Some parts of your brain will shrink. These parts are primarily associated with learning and other complex cognitive activities. (Might explain why I struggle helping my kids with their homework?)
- In some brain regions, communication between neurons may become less effective. (Is this why I am sometimes slow to get a joke?)
- Blood flow in the brain may decrease. (So, maybe I'm not as sharp as I used to be?)
- Inflammation tends to increase with age. (Is that why I feel a bit foggy?)

It's not all bad news though. The ageing brain seems to become better at non-linear and creative thinking, which might explain why we tend to be attracted to more artistic pursuits as we age.

All these changes are natural, but science has proven that fuelling and exercising your brain in certain ways can help protect against abnormal deterioration, and help you function more confidently in life.

a healthy and positive mindset towards ageing literally lengthens your lifespan by more than 7 years.

Matt: This makes me think immediately about the growing number of people supporting parents who have dementia. I'm so glad you mentioned that diet and exercise are being shown to offer protection, because the fear of this disease is probably one of the biggest concerns many people express when we talk about ageing.

Susan: I've seen this with the parents of some friends. Dementia, and particularly Alzheimer's disease, seems to hit suddenly, but it's been silently affecting these people's brains for many years before we see symptoms like memory loss, difficulty with language, loss of problem-solving skills, and just an overall inability to manage the activities of daily life. We probably all know someone who has been affected by it, or someone who is caring for a loved one who can no longer run their affairs without help.

At time of publication of this book, dementia was the seventh leading cause of death and one of the major causes of disability and dependency among ageing people around the world. We're living longer, so it's not surprising that more people find themselves living their last decades with these diseases. From midlife, our risk of dementia doubles every 5 years. That's motivating enough for me to make some conscious efforts to put myself in the best position for a mentally healthy future.

Matt: Pretty scary statistics!

Susan: Even if you are lucky enough not to have the higher genetic risk for such diseases, there are things we tend to do to ourselves as we age that reduce our cognitive reserve, and this is something we can control by being proactive in our strategies for mind care. The first challenge is being willing to get out of our ruts!

Older people can get stuck in their ruts

It appears that, as we age, there can be a tendency for our mental world to get smaller. You hear people say, "He's become very small-minded." "She seems to be obsessed over this one issue." "They can't see the other side." "They always need to be right."

And it is true – there is a tendency for your mental world to get smaller as you get older. Most people are less and less exposed to different people, opinions or perspectives. There's also a tendency to bunker down into routine, visiting familiar places and doing the same things throughout the day. Even though neuroplasticity means it should be possible for us to keep learning new things and adapting to change throughout our whole life, if we get stuck in ruts, we're not going to stimulate new neuron growth. In fact, we're promoting the shrinking of our brain instead. Holding lots of complex things in mind becomes more and more difficult, which increases stress. Some people report feeling anxious when they are faced with something they haven't done before. This all leads to those resistant behaviours we often associate with older people.

Matt: Change can definitely feel harder as you get older.

Susan: And even though I'm saying all this, here's something embarrassing: I avoid self-service checkout registers at the supermarket! I'll wait 20 minutes longer if it means a person will take my groceries, scan them and put them in bags for me, just like the good ol' days. I know it's ridiculous. It's not that hard to scan and bag your own groceries, but you'd think someone was trying to take my children away from me!

As I entered my 50s, I certainly noticed my growing desire for the comfort of routine. Work travel became far less appealing, and even the smallest computer system change became something I'd curse over. Moving house when I was 50 nearly did my head in. So much to navigate – new utility connections, bureaucracy to deal with, juggling many detailed tasks. I hadn't done that for at least a couple of decades.

This is the power of a comfort zone, and by the time you hit mid-age, you'll have created heaps of them. Routine is great for certain things. Repeating something over and over ensures your brain lays down pathways to make that process really easy. If it didn't do this, we'd have to learn how to drive a car every time we got in it. But the flip side is, we often find it really difficult to break some of those habits or ruts we have fallen into. Change inevitably feels harder as you get older, unless of course, you make a habit of shaking things up regularly.

Chapter 24

The Challenge of AI

Matt: I wonder how we'll cope with some of the big changes like Artificial Intelligence? I can't resist diving down this rabbit hole for a bit, if you'll humour me, Susan. In the next 5 years, AI will profoundly impact our workplaces and personal lives. The future is both exciting and uncertain, and while we can't predict all the changes, it's clear that AI will be a significant driver of transformation.

In the elite sport environment where I work, AI is already revolutionising data processing to provide real-time feedback and predict future performance outcomes with incredible accuracy. I recently watched a documentary on advanced brain surgery that showcased how AI is pushing the boundaries of medical technology.

As with all high-level technology, AI brings both amazing benefits and potential downsides. The internet and mobile phones serve as prime examples; they have revolutionised access to information and connectivity, yet they also come with pitfalls such as the dark web and the distraction of constant notifications. We already know how much this can impact our sleep and create isolation. Compared to that, the change we are about to experience is unprecedented. Unlike our parents or grandparents who gradually embraced technology, we are witnessing rapid advancements. Many people have already been made redundant in the tech industry, and other occupations are beginning to feel the effects as AI becomes integrated into various fields.

We are constantly being forewarned about the significant changes AI will bring. Embracing the positives can be difficult, because of the ruts you talk about, Susan. Our behaviours are entrenched through years of subconscious conditioning. Consistently finding value in these changes will be challenging, as they will be entirely new experiences and we don't know where it's all heading. However, the opportunities are immense. Access to knowledge will be greater than ever, especially when it comes to new ways of enhancing our wellbeing.

In modern life, we have unprecedented access to unhealthy food, leading to widespread obesity, type 2 diabetes, and autoimmune diseases. Conversely, we also have more access to health and longevity resources than ever before. AI will present choices, and it will be up to us to seek out the positives and leverage these advancements for our benefit. While the threat to jobs is real, so too are the opportunities for growth and improvement.

As we navigate this new environment, my own experience with AI has been eye-opening. Initially, I was blown away by its capabilities, but over time, I've understood that the quality of the questions you ask determines the value of AI's responses. Your curiosity and desire to expand your understanding of life can be significantly supported by AI, but it requires active engagement.

If you're of a certain age, it can be tempting to ignore these new technologies and hope they won't matter so much in the second half, but I think that will just make life harder in the long term. Being willing to open our minds and learn new things helps us stay relevant and engaged in a changing world. The future with AI can be viewed as a threat, or we can face it as an adventure.

I believe that embracing changes like this can make us better in lots of ways, not just the information gained. As you say, Susan, the very act of being willing to learn makes our brain healthier. And let's remember what won't change: our need for human connection. AI can't offer a comforting hug, share a laugh over a silly joke, or provide the deep empathy that human interactions bring. Human connection remains the cornerstone of wellbeing.

Susan: Great points, Matt. You've had so much experience in recovery programs, working with people who have experienced dramatic changes due to physical or mental injuries. Any lessons in how they cope?

Matt: Those experiences have shown me that, while adapting to change can be extremely challenging, embracing new behaviours can lead to an improved quality of life. Improvement requires change; however change is often awkward at the beginning. Not only do we experience confusion and resistance in ourselves, those around us who are accustomed to our established patterns also push back.

Sustaining changes, such as quitting drinking, starting to exercise, or eating healthier is also difficult. After a few weeks of new habits, temptations like chocolate or a bottle of wine can test our resolve. In short, the biggest lesson is to embrace this change and find how it can make you better. Just like teaching your grandma how to use a mobile phone back in the day, make it fun and accessible. The future with AI is an adventure – let's embrace it together and share your wisdom to enrich not only your own life, but the lives of those around you.

Susan: Thanks Matt, I enjoyed that journey down the AI rabbit hole. There's no doubt that talk of AI is everywhere we turn now. I can see you've been thinking deeply about it. This is another interesting shift I see in many people as we age; we tend to spend more time in our internal worlds.

*embracing new behaviours can lead to
an improved quality of life.*

Chapter 25

Hanging Out in Your Mind Garden

Susan: While this is not the case for everyone, for many people, the second half is more likely to be a time when they're called to introversion. It could be that they have more time on their hands to dive deeper into topics that interest them. I know some people who started reading voraciously, after rarely reading a book during their first half. Some people simply become more comfortable being alone and choosing solitary activities, no longer craving the external stimulation they sought in their youth. Others find that activities they formerly engaged in are beginning to lose their shimmer, and previous interests begin to fade away.

For many of us, values will often come up for review. You see this in people who start rehashing events or trying to understand things that happened some time ago. I see quite a high proportion of men cracking open the door to reflect on their past. Often, it's motivated by a desire to deepen their self-awareness, and deal with parts of themselves they feel have held them back from embracing a full and happy life. We've covered some of that in Section 6 on emotions, but it straddles both topics, because there are often mental health consequences when we ignore how much our mind, and the way we think, drives our behaviours.

The fact that the inner world seems to command more attention in midlife is a positive thing. It may be difficult to face your mental state and do the work, but this is a time in your life when being forced to re-imagine yourself, and dream about something new, really fits in. It's actually very empowering.

The bottom line is that you're going to be hanging out in your mind garden a lot more. Don't you want it to be a place you enjoy visiting?

Matt: I certainly do. Susan, as you said earlier, you've been guiding people for decades in their efforts to cultivate their mind garden, and one of your books is solely on this topic. Tell us how we can approach this in midlife.

Susan: We've been talking a lot about things that can happen to our mental health and happiness when we ignore this aspect of ourselves. While not all the risk factors we've discussed will affect every person, I doubt anyone would reach their later years with great cognitive powers unless they are taking intentional steps to care for their mind. These are the people who've adopted a Mind Training Regime, and anyone can do it.

A training regime is very well accepted when it comes to your body and physical health. The good news is that all those positive choices for your body will also benefit your brain. But there are additional ways you can protect and optimise your mind that are simple to add into your life.

Before we talk about how to build your own Mind Training Regime, let's run through some essential facts.

Your brain is a highly trainable instrument, and it's no different to other parts of your body. If you want to grow your shoulder muscles, you work out with regular exercises and you get stronger. You can see your muscles build bulk and get toned. It's exactly the same in the brain. If you had a brain scanner at home, you'd be able to see which neural connections are getting stronger, and which are getting weaker from lack of use. But all you really need to know is, the more you do something, the more you strengthen the connections between the relevant neurons. Your brain starts to prioritise these pathways, meaning the actions become easier and more natural. The opposite is also true; the less you employ your mind on something, the weaker your brain pathways become, and the harder that task becomes.

Maybe you were an A-grade maths student at school, but if you haven't kept it up, you might find the maths required for your retirement plan leaves you feeling like a dunce. There's research in many areas showing physical changes in the brains of people who practise something regularly, for example playing the piano or learning a language. But this principle doesn't just apply to practical tasks. If you worry or ruminate about something every day, your brain will wire up to become very good at that too. Then you'll find it difficult to stop, not just because the neural pathways are now so strong, but because the time you've spent training your brain to worry means you've neglected training your brain in other things. Just think about how often you're in the middle of a task, then get distracted by something on your phone. You're training your brain to seek distractions, rather than training it to remain focused.

Matt: So, the saying 'use it or lose it' is true!

If we don't start losing some of our bad habits and using some new ones at this time of life, we could miss out on the full potential of our second half.

There are so many great comparisons to physical fitness training here. It's really quite similar.

Susan: Yes, we've been bombarded with education about our physical health and fitness for years. We know that a combination of aerobic and weight-bearing exercise makes for the best overall fitness. You only need to visit a gym to know how well this message has been embraced. People show up regularly throughout the year to keep on top of their fitness. They are proactive about it and don't only do it when they have a 'problem'. Instead, they do it to maintain a healthy level of fitness. We need to adopt the same approach to our mind, because you're right, Matt, if we don't do this, we will miss out on so many things that remain possible in our second half.

Here's how I structure my Mind Training Regime, and there are lots of suggestions of exercises that people can experiment with to build their own.

Mind Training Regime

Chapter 26

The Foundation – Self-Awareness

Susan: Self-awareness is simply about knowing yourself on every level: your thoughts, your values, your areas for growth, your triggers, your strengths, what you stand for. When you understand how all of that plays out and whether it is in alignment with how you live your life, you empower yourself for change.

Matt: Most of us have spent a big portion of our lives with the blindfold on, oblivious to how our own thoughts and behaviours have contributed to the life we are experiencing.

Susan: A friend recently shared over lunch that now, in his 50s, he's adopted the 'Am I the A-hole Here?' test. He went on to explain that, for most of his life, he only saw other people's faults in any situation: that they did him wrong, how they were unreasonable in their actions, what they did to him. With growing wisdom and the benefit of retrospection, he now sees that, in every situation, he also had a role. His new resolve led him to take responsibility, and he's even gone as far as apologising for past regrets. Most importantly, he's discovered a new level of happiness.

Matt: Do you think we get better at self-awareness as we age?

Susan: Self-awareness can head in one of 2 different directions:

1. You come to know yourself better, warts and all, and recognise the patterns that have played out through your lifetime, or

2. You miss the lessons on offer and remain unaware of your patterns and their impact on yourself and others and they become more entrenched.

I think it's pretty self-evident that self-awareness is very empowering, but it does take effort and a willingness. If you're ready, here are a few simple ways to get started.

Questions & Reflections

When you ask yourself questions and pay attention to the answers that arise in your mind, you will often be surprised. Deep down, we already know our needs, our desires and our limiting thoughts. This exercise encourages you to really listen to those authentic responses. Here are some suggested questions to get you started.

- *What are the values you like to live your life by?*
- *What do you stand for?*
- *What are your strengths?*
- *What are you passionate about?*
- *Where are your areas of growth?*
- *What are your triggers? (things that frustrate, annoy or upset you)*
- *How do you know when something has upset you? What are the signs?*
- *If something has upset you, how difficult is it to let go thinking about it?*
- *How busy is your mind?*
- *Can you focus your mind?*
- *What thoughts occupy most of the airtime in your brain?*
- *Where's your mind right now?*
- *What do you get distracted by?*

- *What are the patterns that you keep playing on repeat in your life?*
- *What's the thing you constantly whinge about?*
- *Where are you sabotaging your own success?*
- *Where do your thoughts and behaviours contribute to the experiences you are creating in your life?*

There are many more questions that you could explore. And here's a tip for expanding the impact of this exercise: write the answers down as they arise in your mind. Often the act of writing the words and seeing them on paper will take you even further in your growing self-awareness.

Real-Time Self-Awareness

When you find yourself having a reaction to something (either positive or negative), be curious and ask yourself:

- *What am I reacting to here?*
- *Is my reaction helpful or unhelpful to the situation?*

Matt: Our brain is wired to protect us, not just from sabre-tooth tigers, but also from people's perception of us and how they treat us. While this is totally understandable, it often leads to poor behaviour, lies and playing the victim. When we operate from the assumption that others don't like us, or even the reality of them criticising us, our brain activates our ego into protection mode. While we have no control of what others think of us, a peacock dynamic kicks in, and our behaviours become quite inauthentic and dysfunctional. I have never met a person who hasn't done this, but it does seem to be more prevalent in men.

I certainly experienced this during different stages of my life, particularly as a head coach. At times, I forgot that my genuine self was far more influential than pretending to be someone who was more important. Placing how you want others to value you above your own values leads to this battle between your authentic mind and your ego, and you end up living a lie.

I agree, Susan, self-awareness is the fundamental solution to this. If you are unaware of the power of your ego to bring a dysfunctional approach to life, genuine happiness will be fleeting, and you just can't experience that deep sensation of love for life, family or amazing adventures. I say this from personal experience, and I know the work you share here will help your best self to re-emerge.

Susan: Once you start your self-awareness journey – and it is a journey – your Mind Training Regime will be made up of 3 different types of mind training practice:

1. Mindfulness Practice
2. Mindset Practice
3. Mind Skill Practice

Chapter 27

Mindfulness Practice

Susan: The average person has more than 70,000 thoughts and 12,000 internal conversations going around inside their head every day. You probably aren't aware of most of it, but stop now and close your eyes. Sit for 2 minutes, simply watching any thoughts come up. There's a reason it's called the monkey mind! Your brain playfully throws up relevant and irrelevant thoughts in an endless chatter with itself.

Matt: I'm thinking about what I'm eating for lunch, the email I have to return, something I'm looking forward to on the weekend, a person I'm worried about … and that was just in 30 seconds!

Susan: Mindfulness is not about emptying your mind of this chatter. Rather, think of it as the opposite of mindlessness. Mindfulness switches on your brain and turns off the autopilot. Being mindful means being alert, switched on, focused and present. Mindfulness improves your mental stability, enhances your awareness, and enables you to better focus your attention.

When you are in a mindful state, it becomes easier to change and grow, and life becomes much better. But the benefits don't stop there: your memory improves, learning becomes easier, your connections deepen and enjoyment skyrockets. Mindfulness is linked to new neuron growth, overall brain health, positive emotions, improvements in physical health and immunity, and improvements in decision-making, memory, creativity, and the quality of relationships. If that isn't enough, research also reveals many potential benefits of mindfulness for reducing the risk of age-related cognitive decline. Around 20 minutes of practice a day, integrated into your life, will deliver the benefits mentioned above, and more.

Matt: Okay, so how can we tame these busy minds?

Susan: Mindfulness involves these 2 steps:

1. Training the Awareness
2. Training the Attention

Let's start with **Training the Awareness**.

You may think of awareness as our ability to notice things around us. You become aware that a cloud has passed in front of the sun and it's now cold. You hear an alarm go off and become aware that it's time to get up. But you are also able to notice what is happening within your own mind. Mindfulness training is undertaken to heighten this ability to observe your mind. This means becoming aware of arising thoughts that steal your attention away from the present.

Most of the time you may not be aware of the activity in your mind. You may not notice what thoughts arise in reaction to a situation, or where your mind wanders when you're waiting for someone. When I'm looking for my phone when I'm talking on it, I'm just not present. People call it their 'senior moment', but it is nothing more than a mindless moment. Unfortunately, it appears we have lots of them. A Harvard University study by psychologists Matthew Killingsworth and Daniel Gilbert, revealed that the average person spends 47 percent of their day on autopilot, doing mindless activity without thinking, and being largely unaware of their surroundings or internal emotions. No wonder many of us can't remember someone's name or what we did yesterday! We're are hardly ever 'here'!

Living life on autopilot is unfulfilling. Worse, you will act unconsciously, and that's a recipe for regretting your actions later. Strengthening your awareness is the first step to becoming mindful, and it's something you can become better at with practice.

Start by building the ability to observe the thoughts, reactions and filters that arise in your mind in real time, as you are experiencing them. It is often a lot easier to see these things after the event, but in order to make choices about what gets your attention, you need to see things as they are unfolding in real time. For this, you need to develop 2 skills:

1. Watching the thoughts as they pass through your mind; and
2. Familiarising yourself with thoughts that typically tend to capture your mind.

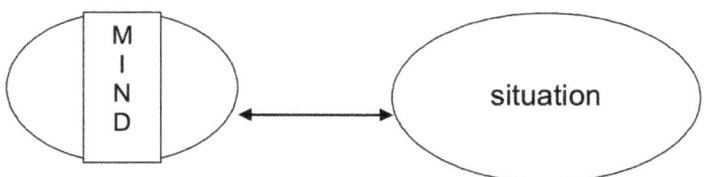

The first step is to be aware of what is passing through the mind and be aware of the potential for these things to filter or distract from the reality of the situation.

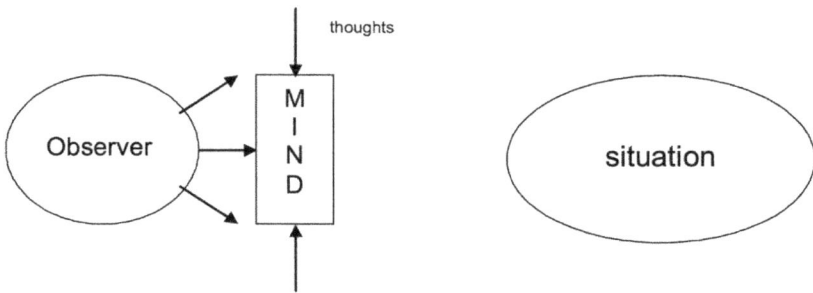

Watching your thoughts is an interesting skill. Initially, you'll struggle to actually see a thought when it happens; but when you literally tell yourself to be the Observer, you'll start being much more aware of the activity in that monkey mind. You'll be able to reflect back and recognise what thoughts you had after you've acted on them. The goal of practising being the Observer is to become better over time at noticing thoughts as they actually arise. Believe me, this is a skill and an extremely empowering one.

You will also notice that there are particular thoughts or reactions that tend to grab your attention more than others. Maybe you are constantly re-running past events, or you have an inner critic who always says you are not good enough. Watch for these patterns of thinking, because it's often these thought patterns that limit your success or keep you stuck in uncomfortable ruts. Once you notice what they are, you have a choice about whether to keep giving them attention, which is why training the attention comes next.

> ## Be the Observer
>
> *Develop this ability to notice your own thoughts by simply asking yourself questions like:*
>
> - *Where is my mind right now?*
> - *What am I thinking right now?*
> - *What thought did I have before I acted that way?*

> ## Noticing Patterns
>
> *Many of our thoughts flow through on autopilot, especially the habitual ones that we have over and over again. By observing them, you can start to see which patterns are helping you live a full life, and which ones are hindering it. You'll also notice that most of the actions or behaviours you want to change are triggered by patterns of thought that make the change difficult.*
>
> *Familiarising yourself with your patterns is not an exercise of deep analysis or complex reflection. Sure, some people will benefit from expert support to deal with the patterns they notice when becoming more mindful; but in general, it's wise to initially simply note down the patterns. Maybe use a journal, so you can see how often the pattern arises and what situations are affected by it.*

> *Don't dwell on them or attach yourself too tightly to them; in fact, sometimes it's even useful to make light of them. I often say, "There's that thought again," as a way of separating me from the thought and letting it pass.*

This reminds me of a conversation I had with Susan not long after I'd been reading Neville Goddard's I Am.

Susan: You've been unusually quiet lately. What's going on in that head of yours?

Matt: I've been reading something that's messing with me, in a good way.

Susan: That sounds dangerous.

Matt: It's about this idea of "I am." The part of us that sits behind the thoughts.

Susan: Go on.

Matt: I realised I'd spent most of my life thinking my thoughts were me. That the voice in my head, the worries, the plans, the doubts and that was my identity. However the book kept pointing to something simpler and a touch stranger.

Susan: Which is?

Matt: That before any thought appears, there's an observer. Before the emotion, there's awareness. And that awareness, the part that says "I am" isn't actually the brain at all.

Susan: So what is it?

Matt: Well that's the thing, the brain is incredible with the key responsibility to keep us alive but it's a record of the past. It scans for danger, runs comparisons and patterns and memories at lightning speed, but it's reactive by design. It responds to real threats, remembered threats, and imagined ones in exactly the same way.

Susan: Which explains a lot about modern life.

Matt: Exactly. We're carrying Stone Age hardware into boardrooms, relationships, traffic jams, parenting, ageing bodies and then wondering why we feel constantly on edge.

Susan: So where does the "I am" fit?

Matt: That's the part that notices the reaction, that can step back and say, I'm anxious right now, rather than I am anxiety. The part that can witness a spiral of thought instead of being dragged into it.

Susan: That feels like a very important distinction.

Matt: It is. Because the moment you can observe your thinking, you're no longer owned by it. Allowing you to choose what to entertain, to challenge, and what to just let pass.

Susan: And that's the second-half upgrade.

Matt: Exactly, when you start operating from the "I am" instead of the noise in your head, something changes. You stop reacting so quickly, you can recover faster and create more freely. For me it enabled me to respond to life instead of being constantly ambushed by it. All I could think was, why weren't we taught this at school? No one ever explained that you could relate to your thoughts rather than be ruled by them. This understanding has profoundly changed how I live, by consciously knowing I can influence my state, rather than being hijacked by whatever feeling or story shows up has opened new levels of creativity, calm, and fun. It's also become one of the most powerful tools I share with others.

Susan: So instead of fixing the outside world, you learned to govern the inside one.

Matt: That's it and once you can watch your mind, you can train it. You can train it and decide what kind of second half you're going to live.

Susan: Sounds like most people never realise that door even exists.

Matt: But it's there for all of us in every single moment and the second we pause long enough to ask, who is noticing this thought right now?

So, let's look at the second component of mindfulness: **Training the Attention**.

This means honing your ability to switch attention and maintain vigilant attention. A large part of this involves paying attention to what you are doing. Do this by focusing on the sense that is most related to what you are doing, for example in a conversation, listen fully when someone speaks to you. When you are moving around, notice your surroundings, taste your food at meals, and really feel things when you touch them. Every time you use your awareness to notice that your attention has drifted, switch it back into the present by connecting to one of your senses. Then give every activity the quality of attention it deserves.

Here are some suggestions for how to specifically train your attention.

Connect to your senses

Your 5 senses are always present, always with your body, but you are often not always connected to your senses. You'll notice that, when your mind drifts and you're thinking about something else, you are not fully aware of what is going on around you. When you connect back to your body through your senses, your mind is in the here and now, perceiving and taking in information right now.

Here are some simple ideas for training your attention. Simply connect to the sense that is most at play when you are:

- *brushing your teeth*
- *washing the dishes*
- *ironing your clothes*
- *driving your car*
- *eating your food*
- *walking somewhere*
- *reading a book*
- *watching a movie*
- *making a meal*
- *mastering your golf swing*
- *painting or doing art*

The opportunities are endless. Pick 3-5 activities you do every day, and use them to fine-tune your attention. When your attention floats away to something else, bring it back to the activity by connecting it to the sense you are using at the time: sight, touch, hearing, smell, taste or general awareness of your body. It is your senses that bring you into the present, so the more often we connect to them, the more mindful we'll be.

Tip: Do these small activities as if you are being tested on them. It can make you more intentional and alert, which focuses your attention more easily.

Matt: The consistent practice of meditation has certainly played a central part in my ability to process things that I had shoved down in my past.

Susan: Meditation is one of the most well-known mindfulness exercises, and it combines the 2 skills we've been discussing: training the awareness and training the attention.

I learnt meditation in my early 20s, when I realised that my mind was busier than a major street intersection. I attended classes in an old church once a week, and committed to practising twice a day for 2 x 20-minute periods. At times it was hard, but I saw the benefits immediately, and my previously stressed out and busy brain literally transformed before my eyes.

Matt: My first meditation experience resulted from reading a book by Phil Jackson called *Sacred Hoops*. Phil was and is the most successful NBA basketball coach in history, leading the Chicago Bulls and LA Lakers to many titles. He got his teams to meditate as a method of accessing their best performance, and it obviously worked. I did some research into the science that existed behind this in 1997 and it all validated the positive impacts.

As a 38-year-old Australian male, head coaching rugby league in the UK, I certainly didn't want anybody to know I was going down the woo-woo path, not even family and friends. So, I went to my local gym at 10am on a week day when no-one was around and, after a workout, I went to the sauna with the intention of sitting in there with my eyes closed and just following my breath for 20 minutes.

As someone who had a pretty high-stress job, not having any thoughts was extremely hard. It's good to hear you say that's not the goal! Fortunately (or not) about 5 minutes into my very first practice, someone opened the sauna door and that ended my meditation. Saunas became a daily practice in my life, as my ability to rest my mind and access creativity and calmness grew.

Fifteen plus years later, this is something that I do twice a day and is central to living a thriving life and overcoming the inevitable challenges we all encounter.

Susan: If someone hasn't tried meditation, or even if they did but haven't continued with it, it's worth exploring. An easy way to put a toe in the water is to try one of the many meditation apps available. You can start with just a few minutes and build up over time, and you can do the meditation at a time and place that suits your lifestyle.

Classes with a teacher offer the opportunity to ask questions and have someone help you make sense of your experiences, motivating you to continue.

There are two myths about meditation I want to dispel:

1. Mediation is not a religious practice, even though some religions such as Buddhism are known for their emphasis on meditation. You don't have to adopt a particular religious or philosophical practice to try meditation.

2. Meditation is not about emptying your mind. That's impossible, but plenty of people mistakenly believe that's the goal. When they try meditation, they say, "I'm no good at this!" and give up in frustration, which is a real shame.

The goal of meditation is to train your brain, and as a result, become more mindful and in touch with your life. Regardless of the option you choose, all meditation generally trains the 2 skills we've been discussing.

> ## Meditation
>
> *You'll be encouraged to observe your mind (Training the Awareness). Meditation is generally undertaken in a quiet place without distractions. This helps you observe what's happening in your mind. One of the first things most people notice is how busy their mind really is!*
>
> *You'll be encouraged to guide your attention to a single point of focus (training the attention). Sometimes it's the sensation of your own breath passing in and out of your body, or it may be a mantra, someone's voice, a specific sound like a bell, or a visual item like a candle flame.*
>
> *By putting the 2 steps together, the goal is to notice when your attention has drifted, and switch it back into the present. You'll only be able to hold that focus for a matter of seconds before your attention is taken away again, and that's completely normal.*
>
> *Remember, this is practice, and that's what builds mindfulness.*

Matt: While being a massive advocate of this approach, I have worked with many people who say this isn't their thing. Maybe it's because just sitting without something to do can feel completely weird and uncomfortable in an age when we all walk around with our phones in our hands.

If people can get past their resistance to mindfulness training, this approach really helps them get in touch with their inner self. When I ask the question, "Who thinks your thoughts?" or "Who experiences your emotions?" people always say "I do". I think it's easier to adopt the 2 steps of mindfulness when doing something more physical. Surfing, fishing, painting, singing or walking alone in nature are just some of the things people can use to process resistance out of their experience.

Susan: Yes, those activities provide a very tangible sensation for people to connect their attention to and maintain their focus in the present. Like all new activities, it's much smarter to start with exercises that help you achieve success and not dive straight into the toughest challenges.

That's why I really focus on daily mindfulness activities, not only when you're first trying it, but also because we can get complacent if all we do is sit in meditation for 20 minutes at the start or end of the day. Let's face it, there's not much point in being clear-minded for 20 minutes, then going to crazy town for the rest of the day! While meditation is a great practice, the real benefits of mindfulness arise when you pepper mindfulness throughout your days.

Daily mindfulness involves the same process as meditation – the mind observing itself and making distinct choices about what it engages with and what it lets go.

Matt: Is it ever too late to start?

Susan: The good news is no! Your brain remains highly trainable your whole life, so it doesn't matter whether you start at 6 or 60. I see more and more meditation groups around for us second-halfers. Not only do you get to learn new skills, you get to practise them in community with others. My friend took up mindfulness at 60, after attending a relaxation retreat and learning how to eat mindfully. She tells anyone who'll listen that it has totally changed her life, her relationship with her husband and her happiness!

Bringing Mindfulness to Daily Tasks

Chances are you already experience moments of mindfulness. You are mindful of other people when lining up to be served. You are mindful of carrying your cup of tea to the couch. You listen mindfully when someone has something important to tell you. You can be mindful of your own emotions: "I feel really angry lately."

Chances are some of these moments of awareness happen by accident. Mindfulness practice is about making these moments intentional and conscious.

Try these exercises to be more intentional about your mindfulness training:

- *Sit quietly and just watch your thoughts. Watch them as if you are watching a movie. Don't get distracted by any of them, but simply observe them and let them go as the next scene of thoughts rolls through.*
- *Spot, as many times as possible, how often your mind is in the future or the past throughout the day.*

> - *Challenge yourself to see how long it is before you notice that your mind has drifted off the task at hand.*
> - *Listen to a piece of classical music. Every time you see a thought, make a mark on your notepad, then return to hearing the music until the next thought arises.*

Matt: Okay, so that's mindfulness practice. What else should I be doing to build my Mind Training Regime?

Susan: Let's move on to Mindset Practice. This one is all about understanding how we see the world, questioning whether our mindsets are still serving us, and refining our perspective for our second half.

Chapter 28

Mindset Practice

Susan: The way we think about the world dictates our interactions with it. That's because mindsets colour and filter everything we see. It's not your eyes that actually do the seeing; it's the complex neural network of views, assumptions and preferences in your brain. When you hear yourself saying things like "Getting older sucks", it makes you approach your years very differently to someone who sees ageing as a privilege. If you want to achieve something or change something, it's not your actions or behaviours that require attention, it's your mindset that holds the key.

Matt: So, where do mindsets come from? Aren't you asking me to change my whole personality here?

Susan: Well, no. The majority of our mindsets come from what we've been told, things we've seen and experiences we've had over the first few decades of our life (and before!). Your brain can only build its story of the world from the information that makes it into our awareness. It starts with our earliest years, when we learnt from our family what was right or wrong, then through school, from our peers, from the news on TV, from books we read and places we visited.

Every single one of us has a completely unique set of neural pathways because of our different experiences. It means we all see the world differently, and have developed different mindsets through which we filter what we see, hear and experience.

Mindsets are more often stories than facts. You can change your mindsets without abandoning your values and beliefs, preferences or goals. What I'm proposing is that we be prepared to suspend our mindsets, take a fresh look, and be open to thinking differently.

Mindset practice is about making more conscious choices about the mindsets we want to take into our second half. First, we need to acknowledge that many of the mindsets that ruled our behaviours and choices in our first half, just won't support a full, happy and healthy second half. Do you have any examples that come to mind for you, Matt?

Matt: Yes, as a young Australian bloke, I saw myself as an elite athlete, full of vigour and potential. But if I'm being honest, much of what I did back then wasn't driven by any kind of deep mindset or purpose. I was caught in what I like to call my 'ego set', a self-absorbed lens through which I viewed the world. Sure, I loved my family and friends deeply, but I carried this internal belief that I was indestructible, a mentality that led me down a path of dysfunction. I mistook reckless behaviour for fun, and I spun elaborate stories to make myself seem like the person I thought I should be, a version of myself far removed from reality.

Looking back, I see how unsustainable this mindset was — physically, mentally, emotionally, and energetically. If I had continued down that path, as many of my friends did, the consequences would have been severe. Some of them, unfortunately, ended up in poor physical or emotional states, some found themselves incarcerated, and others are no longer here at all. I wasn't a bad person, though I didn't realise at the time how much I was harming myself. I never meant to hurt anyone else, but the toll on me was undeniable.

Now, I don't look back on that time with any sense of pride, nor would I ever want to revisit that mindset, but I can't deny the value it gave me either. It created a stark contrast that helped me realise what I didn't want in my life. It also revealed to me the incredible resilience of the human body and mind. Most importantly, it taught me how to craft a better future, one grounded in awareness, growth, and a deeper understanding of who I truly am.

Susan: That's very deep and inspiring, Matt. Mine's a bit simpler. In the first half, I had a 'near enough is good enough' mindset. I'd set out on a 5km walk and throw the towel in at 3kms thinking: *That'll do.* Or I'd decide to eat healthy, but only do it on weekdays and go crazy on weekends. It led to a very inconsistent approach with my health and I realised in the second half I needed more, deciding to follow through on my commitments 100 percent. 'Full commitment' became the new winning mindset for me.

Matt, you've been working with football teams around winning mindsets for decades. How do you translate that into something we can learn in the second half?

Matt: I call this Deprogramming Yourself. Over the years, we've all accumulated certain beliefs and attitudes. Many of these no longer serve us. They are based in the stories we've been telling ourselves about how others see us, and the value we believe we offer. These stories are very rarely based in truth, but rather our assumptions of how others view us, and perceptions we have been taught based on the material world.

We have all met people who are living in fear because of self-limiting beliefs and lies they continually tell themselves. I include myself in this group, and I think you do too, Susan, from what you said earlier.

Here are a few of those lies that I hear often:

- *"I wasn't successful as a young person, so there is no chance in this phase of life."*
- *"I've had my day in the sun, and that has been taken away from me; so now it's time to suck it up and survive."*
- *"I'm too old to get back into a healthy life, and I actually like doing nothing."*

We possess the power to deprogram ourselves from limiting beliefs, and open our minds to new possibilities. It's never too late to embrace change, learn new skills and explore uncharted territories. In fact, this phase is the perfect time to do it, because we know what works and we have the opportunity to turn understanding into wisdom. Wisdom is about what you do with what you know.

The second half is not a time to slow down or withdraw; it's a time to step into the fullness of our potential, embrace the truths this phase reveals, explore where opportunities for growth exist, embark on a real journey of self-discovery, and make the most of time. Embracing the truth is how we navigate this part of our journey, with wisdom, resilience and an unwavering spirit of adventure. It's a time to live life to the fullest, and create a legacy that extends far beyond ourselves.

I like to learn from the people I admire for how fully they live and love their second half. I think we all know someone like this. What do you notice about their thoughts, words and actions? I bet they aren't sitting around dwelling on a past they can't change, focusing intently on their negative health stories, or talking about how 'it's all over now'.

I believe there are a minimum of 5 mindsets you will see in people who are successfully embracing their second half:

1. Gratitude
2. Ageless Curiosity
3. Hunger for New Experiences and Adventures
4. Positive Lens and Abundance Mindset
5. Kindness

Susan: That's a fantastic list. I've never thought about it from that angle, but I agree with all of these. This is going to be fun to explore.

Gratitude

Matt: Gratitude is a real game changer. When you start appreciating the present moment and all the blessings in your life, you begin to shift your focus. Instead of dwelling on what you've lost and what you don't have, you start to see the people and things you do have, and you create more of that.

Susan: Yes! There's a principle of the brain which I wrote in my diary, so I can remind myself constantly: What you focus on grows.

You will literally develop and strengthen the neural network of whatever dominates your thoughts. If you constantly focus on what you don't have, more of that will pile up. If you focus on what you're grateful for, you'll get more of those good things!

It also builds perspective by acknowledging how blessed you are, compared to those in genuine struggle. This is not about putting on rose-coloured glasses and ignoring challenges; it's about focusing on your personal value and what you can bring to your life, and to those you care about.

> ### Gratitude Exercise
>
> *Cultivating gratitude is about incorporating an intentional habit into your life.*
>
> *Why not start a gratitude journal? Before you go to bed at night, write down 3 things you are grateful for. Add to it every day. You may not think it's possible, but give it a try and you may be surprised.*

Ageless Curiosity

Matt: Curiosity has long created the transformative energy that brings joy and success to life. When we think about curiosity, we often think of kids and the young, assuming it's a trait that fades as we grow older. But curiosity has no age limits. It's a timeless quality that lights a fire within us, guiding us towards uncharted territories, pushing us to learn, explore and grow.

We've all encountered elderly individuals whose bodies may show signs of age, but whose sharpness, wisdom and zest for life are truly inspiring. This vitality isn't coincidental. It stems from 2 key factors: a relentless pursuit of learning and a commitment to sharing knowledge with others. Unfortunately, our culture often overlooks the valuable insights of older generations, preferring quick answers from Google or AI. This disregard leads to isolating seniors in care homes, a flawed model that deprives us of their rich life experiences.

AI might provide information, but it can't offer the depth of lived experience. Ignoring this resource contributes to the growing epidemic of psychosocial health issues. This trend is likely to worsen, unless we take responsibility for valuing our life experiences – both good and bad – as sources of learning and growth. Embrace the freedom from societal conditioning and recognise that, regardless of your past, you can learn new things daily. Even if others don't see it, your wisdom has the power to serve and inspire.

Some of the greatest ideas in history came from people who exposed their minds to knowledge from many different subject areas, and allowed their curiosity to roam free. Even more importantly, curiosity feels exhilarating in the moment, and allows you the opportunity to see a future without restrictions or limitations. You might occasionally be wrong about the positive outcomes envisaged, but the pursuit of these dreams alone will elevate your health and wellbeing.

It's like setting off on an adventure without a map, not knowing what lies ahead, and with each step outside your comfort zone, revealing a part of yourself you never knew existed.

Let me ask you this: have you ever stopped and wondered if there's more to life than what you already know? That tug in your heart, urging you to explore, to try something new?

Susan: Yes, often!

Matt: That is the power of curiosity, and your mind asking you to feed it with your energy and intent. By keeping an open mind, by staying receptive to new ideas and perspectives, we unleash a world of possibilities. Imagine a floodgate that is ready to burst open; that's what happens when you open your mind. Suddenly, you're surrounded by new ideas, new experiences and new people, and it's invigorating. I try to make an effort to be surrounded by people of all age groups to feed and encourage this. Spending time with my kids' friends and listening to their perspectives from a point of curiosity and acceptance, rather than judgement, provides some great stimulation for my brain.

It's important to remember what Neville Goddard said, when he distinguished between the brain and the mind. The brain, our organ of thought, is subject to inevitable degeneration over time; however, this process can be slowed through a healthy lifestyle and continuous learning. Your mind, in contrast, has the potential to expand indefinitely if you let curiosity be your compass. It will guide you towards new experiences and true passions, nurturing the childlike sense of adventure that lies within you. This will breathe life into your existence.

Life in the second half can be a tapestry of joy, excitement and fulfilment, all you have to do is take that first step and let the magic unfold.

Susan: Where has curiosity guided you, Matt?

Matt: When I first re-embarked on the journey of curiosity, I was hesitant that it might lead me to getting in front of myself and creating unrealistic expectations of life. Pushing my conditioning of *Don't get in front of yourself, Mate* to the side, has provided access to some of the most wonderful experiences of my life. I would never have believed it, but life has a way of throwing the most unexpected opportunities our way when we are curious.

For me, it all started at an event with a world-renowned guru, an event I had somehow managed to sneak into (don't ask how). There, in the most unlikely of places – the men's urinal, I met the Australian Director of one of the world's best self-help publishing houses. Now a close mate, he started up a conversation as if we were standing at a bar. He was a footy fan and I was the new head coach in town. That bizarre moment set off a chain of events I could never have predicted. Not long after, I found myself in the green room with some of the most inspiring individuals on this earth: Wayne Dyer, Brian Weiss, Esther Hicks, Joe Dispenza, and even the legendary Louise Hay. Each of them became someone I had the privilege to meet, chat with, and learn from, all thanks to that serendipitous encounter at the urinal. These are extraordinary humans, each with wisdom that's truly cutting-edge.

But here's the thing: that knowledge only becomes truly meaningful when you take it beyond the intellectual and into the realm of personal transformation. It's about how you integrate that curiosity and wisdom into the way you live, how you show up in the world and, most importantly, how you evolve as a person. I feel incredibly blessed that this journey has led me to a place where I can turn these teachings into a living, breathing reality in my life. And that, to me, is the most precious gift of all.

But sometimes it's hard to be curious. Falling into the trap of thinking that we know it all, that life has nothing more to offer, is a real male trait. We feel we need it because that's how we care for others and feed the very hungry young guy ego. Showing the vulnerability to say "I don't know" allows the opportunity to learn new things; it also generates excitement to embrace the unknown.

> **Curiosity Tips**
>
> ✓ When you find yourself disagreeing with something, adopt a curious lens. Listen more and ask questions, until you can find common ground.
>
> ✓ Research something you didn't know.
>
> ✓ Attend a lecture or festival you've never been to before.
>
> ✓ Find a group or hobby that exposes you to different generations and age groups.

Hunger for New Experiences and Adventures

Susan: I know this one well. As you already know, in the year leading up to my 50th birthday, I decided to become a rock drummer. I bought the kit, all the gear, and created my solo garage band. I'd been playing the 'air drums' since my teens, and had a curiosity about the drums for as long as I can remember. I'd have an urge to fist pump when I heard a good drum solo, and was constantly tapping either my fingers or my feet to a beat. You'd think I might have taken the plunge earlier, but that's the thing … our early years tend to be filled with time-consuming responsibilities: studying, working, raising kids, running a household. It's not that life had slowed down significantly, but I asked myself: *If not now, then* **when?**

As luck would have it, I met a new friend who is a professional musician. He's not a drummer, but this guy can play anything he picks up. He taught me to kick on 1 and 3, and snare on 2, and off I went. I was a drummer!

It lights up my world. I can't wipe the smile off my face when I'm doing it, and I feel a passion inside that I haven't felt in a very long time. Don't get me wrong, I have also thrown my sticks at the wall. Kicking on 1 and snaring on 2 isn't as easy as it sounds, particularly when you're keeping the hi-hat going at a different beat. And that was just week 1.

As it got more complex, I felt hugely challenged. I hadn't been out of my comfort zone to learn and master something like that in a long time. And although infuriating at times, that was also part of the excitement. The interesting thing is, it started to change everything around me. I began pushing myself into the unknown in other areas, my creativity in business went through the roof and my passion for everything escalated. I began to lean into life more.

Matt: That's a great example, and I'm really happy for you. It sounds like a lot of fun.

Being hungry for new experiences, and eager to uncover passions that have long been dormant, will significantly change your internal energy, and impact positively on everyone around you. We tend to shy away from uncertainty, but the thrill of the unknown can keep you vibrant. Midlife is the perfect time to throw off any old and redundant identities of struggle. A sense of adventure is at the core of a vibrant life in the second half. Pursuing new experiences can help propel you forward through that twisting, turning journey and into a new life of real excitement.

You have to give yourself permission to have an insatiable thirst for exploration, a hunger for new experiences, and a new love for life. Step outside your comfort zone and beyond everyday adventures. Dare to take risks and embrace the unknown. Doing stuff that we have never done, or thought we would never do, is the most fun place. Let me share a story with you.

In 2014, I hit a breaking point, following personal struggles and professional challenges. I'd got the sack from a job I loved and had a relationship breakdown with an amazing partner. Everything had turned to shit. I was desperate to escape, to step away from the noise of everyday life and find space to reset, though I had no clear idea what that even meant.

Then one day, almost impulsively, I walked into a travel agent's office. Ask me how I ended up booking a 4-week cycling trip around Cambodia? I've got no fucking clue. It was one of those moments where you just follow an instinct and hope it leads somewhere good. Three days later, there I was, on a flight to Phnom Penh, Cambodia. I had no receipt, no contact information, not even a hotel name, just vague instructions to meet my guide at a small hotel the next day. I had every excuse to be filled with dread, questioning the sanity and the decision-making I'd made.

But for some reason, as soon as I got to Phnom Penh, I felt something shift. Something that told me I was exactly where I needed to be. What a great place and even better people. There was a sense of excitement bubbling inside me, a thrilling anticipation for the adventure that lay ahead. The month I spent cycling through Cambodia's backroads was nothing short of breathtaking. The landscapes were jaw-dropping, the temples and architecture were insane, coupled with a rich and deeply moving history. But it was the people I met, the villagers and the Buddhist monks in the middle of nowhere, that truly left an imprint on my soul. I forged a bond with my guide that went beyond the logistics of the trip. It felt like we were sharing something deeper, something that went beyond words.

The trip ended up lasting 2 weeks longer than planned but, truth be told, when I left Cambodia, I still didn't have a clear vision of what I was going to do next in life. What I did leave with was something far more valuable: a clear mind and a fresh perspective on life. I had learnt the power of service, of human connection, and what it truly meant to show up for others.

That time in Cambodia became the foundation for what would eventually grow into an award-winning wellbeing business, personal coaching and keynote speaking. It reignited my passion for human connection and established the sense of purpose I'd been desperately searching for. That experience didn't just change my life, it permanently shifted it. For the better and forever.

Consciously accessing this state isn't the easiest thing and you might be thinking: *What's the point of all this, anyway?* Well, the benefits are far greater than the thrill of the experience itself. Once you gain momentum, you start to wonder why you were burdening yourself with doubt and worry about things that weren't even real. It's well established that you can create illness through worry and anxiety, so the opposite must also be true. Joy, creativity and passion can create opportunities and improve health.

"We suffer more often in imagination than in reality."
Seneca

By experiencing fun and excitement, we change our hormonal balance. This improves mental clarity, mood, digestive function, immune system and the list goes on. When we embrace new adventures, we embark on a journey of personal growth, resilience and self-discovery. It also opens us up to deep and meaningful connections with others, by sharing experiences with like-minded individuals and providing support for people who are doing it for the first time. Asking for help creates bonds that go beyond age, background and interests. It creates a sense of belonging and enriches our lives in ways we never thought possible.

Susan: Okay, so what are your best tips?

> ## Ignite Your Sense of Adventure
>
> *Do one thing new every month. Here are some suggestions, but the list is endless:*
>
> - *Try a new sport.*
> - *Take singing or dance lessons – join a group.*
> - *Cook a new meal you've previously thought was beyond you.*
> - *Go to a play you've never heard of. Even better, be in a play!*
> - *Holiday in an entirely new destination.*
> - *Climb a mountain and enjoy the view.*
>
> *Whatever it is, let your sense of adventure guide you, and watch as your life transforms before your very eyes.*

Positive Lens and Abundance Mindset

Susan: I have a friend who I have always suspected won the lottery or makes money in some secret scheme. She lives such a rich, full life. She is the first one to join any new adventure and she's just come back from Nepal, having spent portions of the last 5 years living overseas.

I have other friends who live a life of restriction, unable to follow their dreams or do what they want, because they don't have the money or resources. Here's the interesting part;

by her own admittance, the friend leading the full, rich life has way fewer financial resources than the ones who believe they are financially limited. What she has is a positive and abundant mindset, and that dictates the quality of her life.

Matt: If you spend most of your time sitting around talking about your lack of money, love or opportunities, chances are you're not going to have what it takes to thrive in your second half.

Susan: Yes. When you try to build your success on a scarcity mindset, you are often driven by fear, competition or threat. You begin to make trade-offs that are unnecessary. You say things like, "I'm putting it all into the kids now. I can relax later" or "I'll do the things I love when I've paid off the house". Those statements reveal a mindset that assumes you can't have it all.

Too many people delay one desire for another and live to regret it. When you believe you can't have it all, it forces a choice: I'll take status first, then I'll have money, then purpose and passion, then happiness, then adventure. But is this really necessary? Does the evidence really suggest that it's not possible to be successful, fulfilled and happy all at the same time? Or are you looking for excuses not to live to your full potential?

If more of your air time is taken up with complaining, rather than discussing solutions, you may struggle too. It's not entirely your fault if you generally sit on the more negative side of life. Your brain is wired to detect threat, and is very skilled at spotting problems. For the average person, 70 percent of their thoughts are initially negative, and the only difference between a positive and negative person is that the positive person has intentionally chosen to look on the bright side of life.

You can do this too, by simply retraining your brain.

> **Abundance Tips**
>
> - *3:1 ratio – every time your brain throws up a negative thought, balance it by identifying 3 positives in the situation.*
> - *Have a complaint-free week: no complaining in thoughts or words*
> - *When you find yourself negotiating with life, ask yourself: What if I could find a way to balance it all?*

Kindness

Matt: I feel like we've left the most important one till last. I think kindness is a foundation for so many positive things in life. And for laughs! Laughing is a must. Our relationships and connections can boost our longevity – if they feel nourishing. A circle of supportive friends can encourage us to move out of our comfort zones safely.

When we approach middle age, we also tend to turn our mind to legacy issues. How will I leave the world a better place? How can I make a difference to someone's life? What do I want to teach the next generation?

None of the above happens without holding close to the value of kindness. This is simply the ability to put yourself aside and act in real service to someone else (or the collective).

Acting in a kind way feels good, and research tells us that the giver benefits by experiencing more happiness than the receiver.

Susan: Seems like it should come naturally, but many things get in the way of showcasing our kind sides. On a practical level, it's often busyness – not even seeing an opportunity to serve, because we are too caught up in our own to-do lists. This is where mindfulness practice supports this mindset. Acts of kindness don't have to be big to have a huge effect.

> **Kindness Tips**
>
> *Perform one random act of kindness each week. Ask yourself each day: What would kindness do here?*
>
> *Think about how you will leave the world a better place, and do something every day to work towards that.*
>
> *Opportunities for simple acts of kindness emerge every day. Here are some suggestions to get you thinking:*
>
> - *Let someone in front of you in a queue, especially if they look stressed and in a hurry.*
> - *Send a friend a link to a great recipe you know they would love to cook.*
> - *Let someone into the traffic from a side street.*
> - *Hold a door open for a stranger.*
> - *Check on an elderly neighbour.*
> - *Write a letter to a company complimenting their service.*

Susan: You can see a trend here with all the mindsets. It's simply brain training again …

We have many pathways laid down in our brains, based on the way we have thought and acted up until this point in our lives. When you repeat something, you strengthen these pathways. And when you break a habit, the old neural pathway has less grip over you, allowing your mind to seek a new perspective.

It's easy to fall into the trap of thinking you are only training your brain when you do a specific exercise, but you are training it every minute of the day. Whatever gets your attention is strengthened. If you regularly dwell on the thought: *I don't like this activity*, your initial dislike can grow to full-blown aversion, and you'll take all sorts of avoidance action. Imagine instead if you focus on a more productive mindset: *This activity is challenging, but it's good for me because it gets me out of my comfort zone*. This strengthens the brain wiring that leads to more positive behaviours.

Neuroplasticity tells us that the brain is always doing some form of wiring. Your challenge is to make sure you are wiring for the life you want to create.

Mindset Practice is about taking 3 steps. They are simple, but initially difficult to do (that's why we all need to practise!):

1. **Spot it** – notice your mindsets in different situations, particularly limiting ones

2. **Pause** – take a deep breath and bring your attention back to the present, breaking the grip of the mindset

3. **Choose** – if this mindset doesn't serve you, ask what different approach you can adopt

These 3 steps, repeated regularly, will train your brain for the mindsets you want to cultivate.

Matt: That's like a mini 'letting go', but doing it moment to moment. That reminds me of something we haven't talked about that's crucial to mindset change in the second half: letting go of the past.

Susan: Ah, yes.

Matt: A winning sporting team must let go of the mistakes and regrets of the first half of the game, if they are to be triumphant at the final whistle. It's the same in life. We all have regrets and moments when we wish we could hit the rewind button, but holding onto regret is like trying to swim with a lead weight tied around your ankle. They create mindsets that colour our perspective.

Learning to let go of regrets, to see them as lessons rather than burdens, is easier said than done. But when you develop this ability to reframe the lesser moments of your life as opportunities for growth, life becomes a little bit lighter. Letting go of past challenges is not a one-off thing; it takes consistent practice. I think this is a mindset practice, Susan, because letting go allows you to gain a fresh perspective on things, and that's something we need to embark on to enjoy the second half. And to rediscover fun and joy in life.

Susan: A big part of adopting new healthy mindsets is letting go of the outdated ones. We often miss this step, but it's the most important part. Being stuck in the past, unable to let go of grudges and resentment that weigh you down like a ton of bricks obviously isn't helpful. Equally, continually reliving great experiences that you had in your youth can distract you from what you can do. To move forwards with a sense of freedom you need to own your past, while at the same time recognising that it no longer exists.

The past does not define us. We do have the power to create a new narrative for ourselves, and create a story that fills us with joy, purpose and fulfilment. Sometimes, as women, we can hold on a little longer than we need to! But we also do it because we want to learn.

Matt: To absorb every little bit of learning out of the past requires you to take time to reflect on the key takeaways from life:

- *What do you want to keep doing, so you can enjoy life?*

- *What do you want to stop doing, to maintain health and happiness?*

- *What new experiences do you want to enjoy?*

The fun aspect of this is that it's an evolving opportunity to learn from experiences you had yesterday to things that happened decades ago. I probably do this 4 times a year, at the start of every season. It's a short and fun process to remind myself how important the future is.

Forgiving yourself and others for past events is something that has taken me a while to master, as I had completely got the context of it wrong. I used to think that forgiving someone meant condoning their actions, or going up to someone you had wronged and saying sorry. Forgiveness is not about what was right or wrong; it's about freeing yourself from the burden of anger and hurt. It's a gift we can give ourselves, by allowing ourselves to move forward with a lighter heart.

Occasionally a little bit of help from others can be useful, including a friend, a mentor who can guide us through obstacles, or a therapist who can lend an open ear.

Susan: Understanding the concept of letting go has also been a transformative journey for me, allowing a full embracement of the present and all the possibilities it holds. Finding forgiveness and creating a life that is truly fulfilling is a simple process to share, but it requires you to do the work by understanding how you truly feel, how you want to experience life, and what you need to do to cover that territory.

Matt: Okay, I'm dying to dive into the third level of my Mind Training Regime.

Chapter 29

Mind Skill Practice

Susan: Mind Skill Practice is probably best demonstrated through a story. Around the time I began learning to play the drums, I went to a couple of hip-hop dance lessons, instigated by my girlfriend. I loved dance class as a teenager, and thought I'd still have the wiring to master some choreography. Boy, was I wrong! Do this thing with your arm while going in the opposite direction with your leg and pumping your shoulders to a completely different beat was a challenge. Like the drums, it was more of a mental workout than anything else, and I could literally feel my neurons connecting from left to right brain hemisphere and searching for pathways. I was exercising my body, but my brain was getting the real workout.

And that was one of the purposes of doing it, because a healthy and happy mind is one that remains fresh and flexible. When your brain is nourished with new things to practise and learn, it grows new neurons and forms new pathways that can open up new possibilities. As we age, a crucial step in cultivating a healthy mind is to adopt a lifetime practice of stimulating your mind and nurturing its growth.

Matt: You'll see evidence of the decline of the pathways you haven't practised. Even just navigating a government website can become a complex cognitive task! This is why many people have incorporated cognitive brain training into their routines. Whether it's crosswords, sudoku, Wordle or helping your kids with their studies, something that stretches and exercises your brain is critical.

Many people join this new wave of brain training because they hope to slow the decline of their brain. In the body, an unused muscle will waste away, and so will an unused part of the brain.

Susan: As we age, we all complain: "My memory is not what it used to be", "My brain is getting foggy", "I'm starting to lose it". We are told it's a normal part of ageing, but the truth is, it's a consequence of failing to exercise our mind. As work fades into the background and your life becomes less structured, chances are you'll exercise your mind less. In our earlier years, we had challenging jobs and complex tasks that ensured this exercise happened naturally. If you're thinking: *I can't wait to retire and just switch off,* then think again. It will be critical for you to find some mind exercises to compensate for the reduction in mentally challenging routines. Here are some suggestions:

Simple challenges

- *Incorporate a daily activity like crosswords, sudoku or Wordle.*
- *Play games with others – Scrabble, mahjong, Trivial Pursuit – anything that keeps the brain moving.*

> **Learn Something New**
>
> *Take up an activity that requires focus and concentration. As you saw from my hip-hop dancing lessons, anything that stimulates your mind will help.*
>
> *Many people choose a new language or take up an instrument, and research on both suggests they are really good options. But I say, follow your heart and do something you're really excited to try.*

Matt: Okay, so I'm going to get serious about my Mind Training Regime, but I'm worried about the time it takes. How often do I need to train in the 4 levels of Mind Practice?

Susan: Just like when you're trying to develop a regular physical exercise program, it's useful to have a structure and get into a routine. Here is the recommended formula for getting the most out of your mind practices:

- *Aim for 20 minutes intentional cultivation of your mind every day. It's a small investment to make in your success, fulfilment and happiness.*
- *The proportion of exercises should be 50 percent mindfulness, 40 percent mindset, 10 percent mind skill. Self awareness exercises are ongoing.*
- *As often as possible, incorporate your exercises into the things that you already do in your day. The exercises are not very difficult. Like any new routine in your life, your biggest challenges will be remembering to do them, and resisting the pull of your old habits.*

Matt: That's gold. It seems like men and women have more in common than in conflict, when it comes to cultivating a healthy and happy mind.

Susan: Yes, men and women share much on this journey. But I've got a few additional tips for women, and maybe one insight for men. Do you want to hear them?

Matt: For sure.

Susan: So, women, in case you're still tempted to be a superwoman, let's face a couple of facts:

1. Just because you can, doesn't mean you should! Multitasking isn't great for anyone, so women, just because we've been told we're better at it, doesn't mean we should do it. Multitasking trains our brains to be distracted, and it's not even productive. It takes 1.5 times longer to do a set of tasks when you're multitasking. There is nothing better than doing one thing at a time.

2. This too shall pass. I'm talking menopause brain; it's a thing, at least it was for me. Overnight, I was forgetting people's names – people who I knew very well. I also felt foggy. It was embarrassing and frightening. For someone who had always taken pride in her sharp intellect, I was alarmed to watch it disappear into a muddled mess. But it passes. Cut yourself some slack, and enjoy **not** being on top of everything for a period.

And here's my hint for men about what women want.

Matt: You'll be answering a question we find ourselves constantly wondering!

Susan: One of the biggest things women look for from men in middle age (or any age really), is for them to be present, completely in the moment with us and not distracted. We react badly when we sense you are not listening, when you're multitasking while we're trying to tell you something, when you're looking at your phone, or you're visibly caught in a world of thought.

Matt: Uh-oh, I'm recalling a time I called you to talk about the book and I was also scanning my groceries at the same time. I noticed you got off the call really quickly. Is that what you mean?

Susan: Ha! Good observation skills, Matt. In that example, it probably wasn't critical but had I been sharing something with you that was important to me, then yes, that would not have ended well! One of our greatest needs is not to have our problems solved, but to feel seen, important and valued. Your presence is the currency for that. So, if there is just one takeaway from this chapter for men, I can guarantee you that your mindfulness practice will boost all your female relationships!

Section 6

Master Your Emotions

Chapter 30

Riding the Emotional Wave

"I've got a lot to say about emotions in the second half of life," I told Susan. That cheeky grin came over her face again.

Susan: Matt, part of me wants to ask you to step aside and leave this topic to the experts! I don't think men would argue against the suggestion that, generally speaking, women are the more emotional sex.

Matt: On the face of it, I'd agree with you, Susan. I'm sure there'll be heaps of people reading this book thinking: *How on earth do I take advice about emotions from a white Australian male in his second half?* My response would be, "That's a fucking fair question." But the result of growing up being told to 'harden up', is that the global suicide rate is more than twice as high among men than women. Many more will be diagnosed with mental health challenges.

While there are many interpretations around moods and emotions, the surprising truth is that how we feel is the biggest cause of death and disease on the planet. The biggest cause of heart and lung disease, cancer, liver dysfunction and suicide is stress. Stress is how you feel!

Susan: That's a really fair comeback. We're all emotional beings, and as a mother of a son as well as a daughter, everything you say really concerns me. There are undoubtedly differences between how women and men experience and manage emotions, both in the first half of life and the second.

Matt: I think we've been conditioned differently. I believe women understand emotions much better than men, for the simple reason that they are more prepared to discuss how they feel, and adapt their behaviour towards others based on feedback. By the time most men reach the second half, we have learnt to hide our emotional state, and if we are called out for being cranky or miserable, we tend to respond with denial.

For far too long, men have been conditioned to view emotions as a sign of weakness, and we've been taught to bury them beneath layers of stoicism and indifference. "Have a cup of concrete and harden up," they say, a mantra that echoed regularly in my ears throughout my youth.

But I learnt firsthand that this emotional suppression comes at a cost – a cost measured in lost opportunities, shattered relationships, and the erosion of self. I lost a relationship as a 40-year-old because of my inability to navigate emotions. It had nothing to do with a lack of intelligence or will, it was purely due to never being taught what emotions are, and how to integrate them into my best life.

Susan: You might think our conditioning as girls makes us better at handling our emotions, but there's more to it than that. I also lost a relationship earlier in my life, because I wasn't able to navigate a roller-coaster of emotions. So, it seems like we can all be affected by our ignorance of what our emotions are trying to tell us, and none of us want to go through our second half making the same mistakes we did in our first half. But I think there is a big difference between how men and women experience life as emotional beings, and it's important to understand those differences.

Throughout a woman's first half of life, we ride monthly hormonal waves that trigger mood swings, from tear-jerking sadness to high-energy happiness. Energy hits us in the face, and we're often reading the subtle signals between the lines, which can be a curse. Emotions pull us under, toss us around, and turn us inside out. But remember, that's our true nature: to cycle, move, lose, win, be up, be down, be round and round.

Society encourages women to flatline our emotions. But it's not the same as the suppression men experience. If we end up in a crying puddle of tears in the workplace, it's diagnosed as something 'wrong', so we learn to manage those moments as best we can. Hiding them doesn't mean we completely bury them; we'll talk about them for hours with our friends: "I'm feeling so sad, is something wrong with me? I've been feeling it for a week. Am I depressed? Should I be taking something for it?"

One thing I have tried to do (often unsuccessfully) is not label emotions as 'good' or 'bad'. That can create more of a negative impact than the emotion itself. Remember, we are like Mother Nature. You wouldn't go to the ocean and see it in a rough, wild state and exclaim, "There's something wrong with you! What can we give you to make you flat and peaceful?" Nor would you complain to a tree losing its leaves in autumn, "Oh that's not good! It's lasted for 3 months now. How can we get those leaves back on?" We accept these cycles and see they all have a purpose.

Matt: Even with 4 daughters, I can never truly know how it feels to experience emotions that way. Men definitely have strong emotions, but they're generally related to the circumstances we find ourselves in: falling in love, pride in our work, fear of losing, anger at being treated badly.

Susan: I'm definitely not saying men don't feel, but it's been suggested that men have denser nervous systems than women. They're emotionally thicker ... in the nicest possible way.

Matt: Don't worry, it's probably not the first time I've been referred to as thick!

Susan: Biology offers insight into why we feel emotions more than men.[11] We've already spoken about how women have fewer pain blockers. According to studies, twice as much morphine is needed to dull pain for women compared to men. This is because women don't have as many *mu opioid* receptors, which are the ones that bring in the feel-good endorphins to fight the pain.

In the brain, social pain (hurt, rejection) registers exactly the same as physical pain, so this is why we often need a double dose of care to soothe it. (Note to all our partners and exes: this is why we were 'still going on about this', way after you thought it was finished).

Matt: I would never dare say that to a woman! But I think we're more practical. We jump into solving the problem and resolving the pain.

Susan: Well, that might also be explained by physical differences in the brain. The fibres that run between the area of the brain that regulates emotion, and the area that

---

11 - See References 11.

interprets it, are literally bigger in women. This probably explains why men are more likely to get in their heads about issues before they feel the emotions. Women tend to jump to the emotional pain part faster.

Matt: Yes, sometimes I have a delayed reaction with really feeling something. We probably spend too much time in our heads. But I don't want you to feel you have to justify why you are emotional beings. It's not a bad thing or something to be embarrassed by. The feeling of feelings is why women make great healers, mothers, nurturers, peace-makers and lovers.

Susan: Being in touch with the emotions of others is great, but it's a double-edged sword. Women tend to experience more negative emotions, such as guilt, shame and embarrassment. Social anxiety is more pronounced in women too. I believe this is linked to the way we experience pain. When we have social pain, we tend to go inside more, which amplifies emotions.

Hormones also count. Higher levels of testosterone equal less pain. We have lower levels of testosterone compared to men; therefore, the same heartache can feel milder in men and more acute in women.

All these factors explain some of the differences between men and women, but that's just the background to the main emotional show during midlife: menopause. There are really specific things that happen during and after menopause that affect women's emotions.

But before we go there, Matt, I'm really curious to know, apart from the lost relationship you spoke of earlier, what set you on the path of investigating emotions?

Chapter 31

Unresolved Emotions

A wave of sadness and vulnerability swept over me, as I remembered the face of a man I deeply missed.

Matt: I lost my dad, my hero, when I was just 13. For that brief time in my life, he profoundly shaped my understanding of goodness, and the emotional depth required to lead a fulfilling life. It wasn't what he said that stayed with me, it was what he did. One powerful example stands out, one that I absorbed subconsciously but would only come to fully understand later in life.

My dad was my footy coach in Townsville, where I grew up. At the time, I didn't give a second thought to the fact that over half the team were Aboriginal or Torres Strait Islander. My dad drove most of the kids home after training. There were 10 kids crammed into our old station wagon, and each drop-off was as much fun as training. One day, after the last Aboriginal kid was dropped off, James, one of the remaining 4 white kids in the car, made a racist joke. I don't remember the joke, but I remember what happened next with crystal clarity. My dad pulled the car over and calmly said, "You can't say that in this car. You'll need to get out." James burst into tears, pleading to stay; but my dad, without raising his voice said, "You need to get out." He made James walk the 2 kilometres home.

There was no lecture for those of us remaining in the car. Just the quiet consequence of having crossed a line. The next training session, my dad continued to pick up and drop off every kid, including James, without a word about what had happened. In my entire time with him, I never heard my dad raise his voice, belittle anyone, or walk past inappropriate behaviour, no matter how small. He didn't tolerate anything that emotionally hurt someone else, and that included me.

"If you walk past it, Matthew, you allow it into your own life," he'd say. This was the emotional foundation my dad gave me, forged through his own life experiences. He was a man who served in World War II, lost many friends, and had to do the most difficult things to survive. Dad learnt the value of kindness and respect through immense suffering, and in the hardest of circumstances. I didn't realise at the time, but his emotional intelligence became a cornerstone of my approach to life.

It wasn't until later in life, when I faced my own personal challenges in my forties, that I truly understood how this foundation was the key to thriving in the second half of life. I hadn't yet learnt how to harness my emotions to elevate my life, but looking back, I see how my dad's unwavering emotional clarity gave me the tools to build resilience and lead with emotional strength, both in the most difficult moments, and equally in great times. His passing was a huge loss in my life.

But the moment I realised I needed to come to terms with my own emotions was a lot more recent. In April 2024, tragedy struck in an Australian shopping centre. A man, driven by an incomprehensible rage, unleashed violence upon unsuspecting women, leaving in his wake a devastating toll of lives lost. Concurrently, across the country, other women were falling victim to past abusive partners who had somehow slipped through the cracks of justice.

These events not only shook our nation, they also struck a chord deep within me. As the headlines blared and society grappled with this stark reality, it became painfully clear to me that we were not merely facing isolated incidents of violence, but rather symptoms of a deeper societal ailment – the unchecked emotional turmoil that simmers within men and often erupts into destructive behaviour.

Mere days after the April tragedy, I found myself in an elevator with a young woman. Her fear at my mere presence was palpable. Coming on the back of those events, it felt like the first time I was conscious of the fear that women carry daily – a fear born in the shadows of male aggression. In that moment, I made a split-second decision to step out of the lift, sparing her further discomfort.

In the days that followed I had similar encounters, each serving as a poignant reminder of the emotional chasm that divides us. It was in these moments, amid the backdrop of fear and uncertainty, that I began to confront my own journey with emotions. And so, fuelled by a burning desire for understanding, I embarked on a quest to unravel the mysteries of emotion. What I discovered was both profound and complex: emotions, far from being adversaries, hold the key to unlocking a life of depth and meaning.

Susan: That was a powerful experience for all Australians. Not only did it elevate the conversation about violence in our society, particularly domestic violence, it highlighted that emotions unchecked and out of control can be dangerous, even deadly. But being willing to face them, and unravel what they are trying to tell you, can free you up to really live your life. This often comes to the surface during midlife and it's like a genie – once it's out of the bottle, don't try jamming it back in.

Matt: Totally agree, Susan. For most of my life, improvement was limited to getting smarter or fitter. While there's merit in this, it became clear to me that many men in my circle lacked an understanding of how emotions impact wellbeing, a crucial aspect I now work with regularly in my coaching.

I truly believe that the biggest cause of death and disease for humankind is how we feel. Some call it stress, others call it pressure, anxiety, depression, or PTSD (Post Traumatic Stress Disorder). I've seen firsthand how these states are strongly linked to heart disease, cancer, autoimmune disorders and dementia.

Let me tell you about a very experienced and high-ranking ex-police officer I worked with. He was knowledgeable about many complex topics and was also a CrossFit champion in the senior age bracket. In a conversation about the hormonal impacts of stress, I explained how short-term stress can be beneficial for building capacity, but the release of sustained adrenaline and cortisol will negatively impact our physical, mental and emotional states.

He responded, "I not only get it, Matt, I've also lived with this every day of my professional life and brought it home with me. The memory of my work prevents me from enjoying life and doing what I want."

He is the clearest example of PTSD's impact among the people I worked with. He was extremely fit and had been an inspirational leader. He requalified as a high-school science teacher to help kids, yet his emotional state prevented him from feeling functional and safe in the environments he wanted to influence. He got a teaching job immediately after qualifying, but experienced a wave of emotions that kept him from showing up one day.

Despite his challenges, he had covered many lifestyle approaches that I often introduce to others: diet, breathing, mindfulness and sleep. In fact, I also learnt a lot from him in many areas. The turning point came when we discussed building emotional capacities. "Look, this is one thing I do with people that isn't scientifically validated, but has helped me and many others."

"I'm all ears, Matt, but you know if I think it's shit, I'll tell you."

I explained that, just like building physical capacities, focusing on the emotions we want to experience, rather than those we don't, is crucial. By loading ourselves with positive feelings in short bursts, we can turn these into our temperament, and ultimately impact our personality. Consistent effort is key.

"I get it, Matt, but sitting in feelings scares the shit out of me, so I might give that a miss."

We moved on to another topic, and I understood that pushing this approach could easily trigger his past experiences.

About 6 weeks later, he called me. "Okay, Matt, I'm about a month into your process and it's working for me. I need to see what the next level is."

"Which process are you talking about?"

"Your weird emotional capacities stuff. I've learnt to lift the light dumbbells; now I need to put some weight on the bar."

"Didn't you tell me it wasn't your thing? What have you been doing?"

"Matt, I'm an ex-investigator. I listen and remember. I attended your program where you taught everyone the foundations."

"So, why didn't you ask me to help you with it? We have coaching sessions every fortnight."

"I was scared and thought it best to trial it myself. If things went pear-shaped, I didn't want to burden you."

"Holy shit. So, what have you been doing, what results are you getting, and what do you want to move to next?"

Over the next 2 months, he and I worked on my developed processes and how to integrate them into his practices. This collaboration allowed me to build advanced techniques and variety, to promote continual development.

About 3 months later, he invited me to his school to present a nutrition chat to his Year 12 class. Watching him inspire these young people, I realised how lucky they were to have someone with such incredible life experience teaching them, not just curriculum-based work, but also demonstrating behaviours of the highest quality.

As I left, he came up to me and said, "Thanks, Matt. You saved my life." I shook his hand, went back to my car, and cried.

Susan: That's a great story. It must have been very humbling. He sounds like the sort of teacher I'd have wanted for my kids, particularly my son.

Matt: It was a pretty powerful reminder and you can't help seeing it as a gift that some of these emotional challenges surface in midlife.

Susan: Midlife has a way of forcing our unresolved emotions to the surface. A happy second half depends on shedding things that weigh heavily, and unresolved emotions from the past are a major part of that. Many men seem to be on a journey of uncovering their emotions and diving into them during midlife. I watch older guys doing everything from taking their grandkids to school, through to facing their childhood trauma. They seem more ready to embrace all the emotions they avoided in the first half of life.

Matt: I come back to my shoe analogy again. What do you do when you've got a rock in your shoe? The answer is always, "You take your shoe off and take it out." Of course you do, but what if you ignored it? Your body would say, "Well, discomfort didn't work; let's try pain." This would continue to ramp up to agony, until there is a response. I'm now thinking about the biology facts you raised earlier, and I wonder whether men let things get worse before they resolve them, because we don't feel the pain as quickly as women do? We have other reasons for ignoring emotional pain – conditioning, ego, fear, as well as a lack of skills and support. But I want to encourage men to get that rock out of their shoe!

In most situations in our life, emotions provide us with a signal of our state in any given moment of the day. "I'm excited to see my friends." "Work is so boring." "I'm nervous to meet so-and-so." In acute situations, they move us into what should be short-term states of fear, anger or panic, and also peak states like joy, excitement and love. If we were taught to pay attention to these signals, we'd ask the question, "Why do I feel good, and how do I maintain this state?" or "Why do I feel shit, and what do I need to do to feel better?" As simple as this may sound, very few people have been taught to pay attention to these signals until they reach the acute level, and even fewer people have been taught how to build the capacities they want.

I'm with you, Susan. I believe there are no bad emotions. For example, anger and fear get a bad rap, but both are very handy when dealing with injustice or real threats. Running away from a tsunami or stopping someone from smashing windows are definitely helpful responses. But these emotions deplete us, if we stay in them too long. Perceived threat, imagining anxiety, and remembering depression are prime causes of that stress we discussed earlier. And just like the rock in your shoe, if you don't pay attention to them, they will have outcomes that negatively impact your health.

Susan: I remember studying Buddhism in my late 20s, and I really liked how they talked about emotions. They made a distinction between virtuous and non-virtuous emotions. The virtuous ones lead to long-term happiness, and are more focused externally or on others, rather than being self-centred – things we've already talked about like compassion, gratitude, kindness, joy and love, including self-love. The non-virtuous ones usually arise from a focus on yourself and falling into the 'it's all about me' trap: jealousy, self-criticism and fear.

It's interesting that this coincides with a pattern often reported for those in their second half; a tendency to look outward to how they are contributing in their community and what legacy they want to leave. This is more evidence that the second half is the perfect time to let go of the non-virtuous emotions and really boost your experience of the virtuous ones.

Matt, why don't you take us through the process you use with people, because I think that deals directly with the question of how to bring more of the emotions we want into our lives. Together, men and women can learn to harness the power of emotions as a guiding force, steering us towards a life of authenticity, connection and purpose in the second half of life. This allows us to not only positively impact our own experience, but equally those who share our space.

Chapter 32

Building Emotional Capacities

Matt: Building emotional capacities, like physical and mental ones, requires a structured approach. Just as we push our physical limits at the gym or expand our minds through learning, we can cultivate our emotional strength by following a similar process. This involves challenging ourselves, allowing time for recovery, and consistently practising our goals. I take people through something I call the Emotional Blueprint.

In my personal exploration, I started with very complex research which, to a large degree, wasn't helpful. However, when I was able to compare building emotional capacities to physical and mental development, it not only helped me, but also many others who I was coaching individually, tens of thousands of people who came to my business program, and those who read my first book, *The Change Room*. It wasn't about creating knowledge; it was about giving people access to tools that help develop emotional capacities to build resilience, and embrace the amazing things that life has to offer.

It became clear to me that this wasn't just a bloke thing, and it wasn't just a second half issue. So, the approach I developed works for anyone who is prepared to do the work.

It does, however, have more relevance for people in the second half, as they have often been trapped in the emotional void for longer and feel disempowered, unable to find a way out. Men are over-represented in this group, because we aren't as prepared to show the vulnerability that women do with their close friends and networks.

Susan: Chances are we've all accumulated some emotional baggage across half our lifetime – you wouldn't be human if you didn't. If your emotional backpack is loaded down with a bit of resentment, mixed with anger and frustration, carrying those negative emotions into the second half of your life won't serve you well.

Matt: You bet. Just like building physical capacities, it's useful to understand where you are right now. For example, "I'm carrying some emotional baggage that I'd prefer not to," or "I'm getting comfortable lifting more of those heavy feelings that used to weigh me down."

Having the winning game face involves a regroup at half-time to celebrate the things you did well. The goal is to do more of them, realign a few things, and let go of the disappointments, unfair rulings, mistakes and self-loathing. If you take that baggage onto the field, the game is over before it begins.

As a middle-aged man dealing with a relationship breakdown, having my attention drawn to what I didn't want was easy, but it allowed me to perpetuate the emotions of sadness, regret and anger. While I am in no way suggesting that these feelings be ignored, they are signals that should prompt the questions, "Why do I feel this way?" and "How do I want to feel?" Focusing on feeling bad not only strengthens that emotion, but also entrenches the behaviours associated with it.

Sticking with the physical analogy, you need to determine where you are now and where you want to get to, allowing you to plan a process of development. For some people, there's a deeper piece of work to understand where they are now, for example why you may be captured by an addiction, or experience bouts of uncontrolled behaviour. I'm not going down that rabbit hole because that's not my field, and I encourage anyone with traumatic emotions like this to seek professional support.

Having a plan to build physical capacities is very handy, but you must do the work, and it's the same in the emotional realm. Just like exercise, where it's easier to sit on the lounge than to train, it's easier to have the shits or be a victim than it is to be in a state of sustained happiness.

Susan: And here's the other risk, Matt. Some methods used in physical training aren't always super healthy, and they often focus more on how you look. Emotional development is very similar. Consider the middle-aged guy who takes up meditation because his new girlfriend does it, or the woman with the carefully cultivated Instagram account claiming to be a #grateful guru. Genuine emotions are not skin deep.

Matt: Good reminder, Susan. And just in case someone's wondering about my reason for using all these physical analogies, and why I'm possibly overexplaining how emotions work (believe me, I could write a whole book on it), it's primarily due to my own inability to understand them. This was the process I needed to create to help myself, and then ultimately thousands of others. Anyway, back to it ...

There are numerous methods to help build your emotional capacities, with the similarity to physical capacities being that you need to push yourself into a peak state, then have an approach that enhances recovery. Just like exercise, this isn't a process you need to engage in all day. And just like exercise, it doesn't mean you'll feel amazing every second of the day.

The practices in the following chapters are designed to give you access to the states you want to tap into in different situations, from the ecstasy for a loved one experiencing success, to personal challenges and achievements. These are peak states that you're meant to access to navigate situations; but just like sprinting or lifting heavy weights, it's not particularly healthy for you, or those who share your space, if you stay in these states all day.

Chapter 33

The Emotional Blueprint

Matt: Love is at the core of our most meaningful experiences: the people we cherish, the moments that shape us, and the self-appreciation that fuels our journey. Wealth, health and status can enhance these experiences, but without love, they lack depth and meaning. Love is what brings joy, inspiration, connection, and a sense of purpose to our lives.

Learning is what allows us to transform challenges into growth. Emotions like resentment, sadness, dominance or victimhood have their place in our immediate reactions, but when we hold onto them for too long, they drain us – mentally, physically, emotionally and even spiritually. The ability to shift from, "Why is this happening to me?" to "What can I learn from this?" is a game changer. It's not easy, but it's the key to moving forward and truly thriving.

The biggest breakthrough for me? The more I stay present with the feeling of love, not just acknowledging it, but really tuning into how it feels in my body, how I share it, and how I attract it, the faster my learning accelerates. My understanding of who I am, my purpose, my relationships, and the whole human experience has expanded dramatically in a short time.

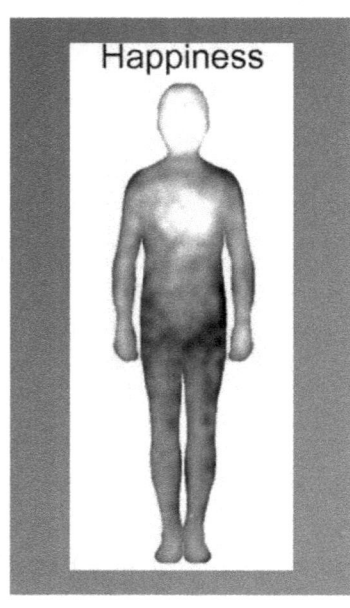

1. Find a Quiet place
2. Close Your Eyes
3. Centre Yourself by Placing Your Attention in Your Gut Area **"I AM Being LOVING"** (1-2min)
4. Move Your Focus to your heart **"I FEEL LOVE"** (2min)
5. Move Attention to Eye Level **"I ALLOW MYSELF TO FEEL LOVE"** (2min)
6. Connect to the **FREQUENCY OF LOVE** (4-5min)
7. **Journal**

This is a process to elevate our capacity for love and higher emotions. After practising it myself and introducing it to a handful of key clients, the results have been nothing short of remarkable. What's surprised me most? Eight of these clients are men who, on paper, fit the stereotype of being more closed off to this kind of work. Yet, after a bit of convincing, they embraced it – and their feedback has been inspiring.

At the heart of this practice is a simple but profound shift: being present with the sensation of love – not just the intellectual concept, but the actual felt experience. Once this clicked, the outcomes were strikingly consistent. It wasn't about reaching a state of bliss (though this will make you feel amazing). Instead, the real magic was in the intuitive insights that surfaced in answer to challenges, clarity around personal experiences, and a deep sense of connection. As Wayne Dyer said: *It moves you from 'no where' to 'now here'.*

When we're stuck in emotions like anger, fear or sadness, our cognitive abilities take a hit. We get distracted, caught up in past regrets or future anxieties, and disconnected from reality. It makes sense, then, that if we rest in the energy of love, something powerful happens – our intellectual capacity expands. Through my own experience and that of my clients, I've seen how this practice unlocks knowledge and understanding we've never accessed before.

Some describe this as spirit. Others call it God. For me, it's simply the pure energy of who I am.

The Practice: Accessing the Energy of Love

This process is simple, yet profoundly effective. Here's how to do it:

Step 1: Create a Space for Stillness
Find a quiet place where you can fully relax with minimal distractions.

Step 2: Close Your Eyes
This reduces external stimulation, allowing your focus to turn inward.

Step 3: Focus on Your Gut
Bring your attention to your stomach. We've all heard the phrase 'gut instinct'. Once you feel centred, repeat these affirmations internally:

- *I am being loving.*
- *I love all of life.*

- *I am being loved by life.*
- *I love who I am and who I am becoming.*

Stay present with this feeling for about a minute. If your mind drifts, simply guide your focus back to your gut and repeat the affirmations.

Step 4: Shift Attention to Your Heart

The heart is where we experience love in its purest form. Affirm:

- *I feel love deep in my heart.*
- *I feel the energy of love soaring through my body.*
- *I feel love for myself and for the special people in my life.*
- *I feel love.*

Rest in this state for 2-3 minutes.

Step 5: Move Awareness to Eye Level

Our brain stores past experiences and knowledge. Here, we give ourselves permission to experience love fully. Affirm:

- *I allow myself to love all of life.*
- *I allow myself to be loving and to be loved.*
- *I accept that I love myself.*
- *I accept that I was made to love.*

Step 6: Connect to the Frequency of Love

This part of the process varies. Some feel love as a flow of energy from the base of the spine to the top of the head,

> others as a tingling sensation. The key is not to force an expectation, just allow yourself to sink into the energy of love in your own way.
>
> **Step 7: Stay in This Energy**
> Remain fully present in this state of love for 4–5 minutes. If thoughts come up, gently shift your focus back to the energy.

When finished, gently bring your awareness back to your body and slowly open your eyes. I strongly suggest you have a journal nearby and write down whatever comes to mind. It's important that you don't feel the need to make things up. If nothing profound arrives in your thoughts, just quickly record how you feel.

When to Practise
The best times are first thing in the morning or before bed, but the most important factor is choosing a time when you can relax without falling asleep.

What to Expect
You don't need to be exact with the affirmations, what matters is the state of experiencing pure love. Most people experience a flood of insights and breakthroughs in the hours or days that follow. Some have major epiphanies in the middle of the process.

Just like physical training, emotional training requires recovery, and I think of it as the missing piece. The goal isn't to be in a constant state of love, but to access and embody this emotion whenever needed. Think of it as having a skill at your disposal, ready to be used.

Personally, I've used meditation since 1995 to accelerate recovery after peak states, such as sitting in an NRL head coach's box for 13 years. However, doing it once a week had little impact. I needed to integrate exercise and fun family time. Friends of mine use other methods like surfing, painting, fishing, yoga and walking in nature. The key is finding what helps you return to equilibrium.

Recovery isn't only required after emotional challenges — it's just as crucial after experiencing ecstasy, joy or extreme excitement.

Through consistent practice, you build the capacity to summon emotions like love, inspiration and freedom at will. You won't walk around perpetually in these states, but you will have the ability to tap into them as needed, much like a strong person can lift heavy objects or a knowledgeable doctor can diagnose a condition. By intentionally developing these emotional capacities, you enrich your life and enhance your wellbeing.

Susan: I don't mind the idea of us all walking around in perpetual love! But yes, strengthening your emotional muscle means being able to return to these states at will. This sounds like emotional resilience.

Chapter 34

Emotional Resilience

Matt: Emotional resilience is often discussed without a full understanding of what it means. Suggestions such as developing a strong support network, practising self-care, and maintaining a balanced perspective on life's challenges are all shared as key essentials. While these are important aspects of our lives, they do not address the essence of resilience.

Resilience is our ability to bounce back to our existing capacities. In a physical context, when you train to fatigue and then rest, you return to your pre-existing capacities. By doing this consistently, your abilities slowly improve. Mental ability is the same: you study, then rest. Eventually, the information turns from understanding into knowledge. The resilience measure in both these areas is that when physically or mentally exhausted, after resting, you return to your pre-existing state. While there are ways to accelerate recovery, you can't shortcut the step of doing the work – that's what elevates your resilience.

Emotions are the same. Recovery is vital, but you need to learn to focus on the emotional abilities you want to serve you in positive ways, and work on building these capacities. As a public speaker who often presents in challenging environments, like correctional facilities or mines, I want to be inspirational and enthusiastic, because that helps people engage with my content after challenging days at work or prior to tough shifts. While self-care and support are helpful, being in an empowered state requires me to have immediate access to the emotions of passion and inspiration. To do this, I worked on strengthening these emotions.

By understanding and developing your emotional capacities, you can navigate life's challenges more effectively and embrace the amazing experiences it has to offer. Remember, just like with physical fitness, emotional fitness requires effort, commitment and a willingness to push through discomfort to achieve growth and wellbeing.

Susan: I keep being reminded of the principle, what you focus on grows. It's true of mindsets, physical capacities and emotions. We want the positive and virtuous emotions to dominate our life, however we can't always get there, unless we fully recognise and embrace negative emotions for what they tell us. These so-called 'negative' emotions happen for a reason. Rather than pull away from them, I would encourage people to consider whether this is an amazing opportunity for emotions like anger to be seen, felt and healed.

Matt: Susan, it's important that we reinforce that: all emotions have their place. Anger and fear can be useful in certain situations, but we need the skills to recognise when they are overstaying their welcome. Learning self-awareness to identify and address these emotions before they lead to chronic stress is crucial.

When you experience tragedy or loss, which in the second half are inevitable, self-awareness allows you to frame your emotional state around care. If you didn't care, you wouldn't feel sadness or grief. If you thought your response or actions were acceptable, you wouldn't experience guilt or insecurity. These emotions can be super helpful if you recognise them.

Susan: All of those tips and exercises are useful for women, and to be honest, Matt, you've simplified things for me in a really positive way. I often get lost in the complexity of my own emotions and greatly benefit from simple paths out of them. However, I think there are some very distinct nuances for women that I'd like to address.

The Wise Woman phase comes into being because a woman has fully integrated all of her past experiences, learnt to forgive herself and others, and reached a place of acceptance where she doesn't need to judge those experiences as 'good' or 'bad', but simply agree that she wouldn't be who she us without them.

Your past has so much power over your life, if you haven't fully owned it. Trying to hide it from others, and also from yourself, simply doesn't work. Anything we relegate to the shadows takes on a stronger and more powerful life of its own. In fact, you are more likely to create a future that looks pretty similar to your past if you haven't fully integrated the experience.

Past emotions are yearning to be seen, felt, witnessed and transmuted. They'll show you what needs to be cleared out to fully step into your Wise Woman phase. Instead of letting them lie dormant as a low buzzing frustration, they are experienced as a feeling of rising power from within you. You're ready to bloom ... but bloom into what? That's yet to be discovered. What you're hearing might be that little voice of intuition, the experience you have built over a lifetime, converted to wisdom. It's saying you're ready to design the next phase of your life, ready to launch and be shared with the world. But before you bloom and redesign, you might need to make peace with your past.

Matt: "If I had my time again ..." The benefit of retrospect. Men get that too. I can relate to everything you are saying.

Susan: I feel like women experience this stronger in midlife. We are constantly evaluating: maybe you would have made different decisions, parented differently, been a better partner, changed career paths. But you didn't. And that was perfection. Use it all as motivation for how you'll play the second half. It's never too late to have the life you want.

All these emotions you are experiencing can be used for transformation, not destruction. One of the reasons they emerge is because you find yourself in a big void between the old way and a new way you can't even imagine yet. Yes, that's scary, but the emotions are signs that intuitive wisdom is coming through. You'll only maximise it if you make peace with your past. Here are some tips to consider.

Feel the pain, grieve what you've lost

What are the sad things in your life so far that are keeping you stuck? Chances are you've pushed down the pain for half your life. It's time to give those emotions space and feel them. Express whatever wants to be shared. It's not easy, but you'll feel so clear afterwards.

Forgive others ... and yourself

Maybe you see others being the cause of your pain. Maybe they were. When we forgive them and acknowledge that the acts were a reflection of their pain and not us, we release ourselves from the past.

> *Maybe you're ashamed of things in your past. Remember you did the best you could with the wisdom (or lack thereof) you had at the time. Embrace every single part of you – even the ugly.*
>
> **Get out of victim mode. Nothing good happens there!**
> *Can't have your best life because of time, money, your ex, your health, your daughter-in-law …? I get it. But this is a sure path to never getting what you want. Until you realise that you have full responsibility over your life, it will be hard to make changes. Don't let anyone (particularly ghosts from the past) get in your way.*

Matt: These are great tips for men. We're particularly good at playing the victim. We also do too much of the opposite, taking responsibility for things that weren't ours to own.

Susan: Yes, you guys always want to jump straight to 'fixing' things.

Matt: So true. It's really deeply wired, but I think I'm beginning to learn where to use my fixing energies, and when to stand back and allow nature to take its course. Speaking of which, you can't leave us hanging any longer.

Chapter 35

Emotions and Women

Matt: I don't know whether you're avoiding the topic or deliberately making me wait, but it's time we talked about menopause again. I know other men will thank me for pushing this, because we need to learn as much as we can about the experiences of our partners, friends, colleagues and family members. Maybe if we understand it better, we'll not only be more supportive, we might also make better choices in our own lives.

Susan: That's great, Matt, and I'm happy to answer all your questions, from my perspective anyway. But you'd be surprised how many women are just as confused by the emotional turmoil of menopause as men are. That's my real motivation to lay out my experience, in the hope that women will discover how to move into the power of their second half, rather than feeling lost.

When we hit menopause in midlife, we experience a whole new hormonal phase, when emotions we've never previously experienced can suddenly flood through our body. I know women who were always relaxed and happy, suddenly talking about feel melancholy, and others who were the calmest women I knew, suddenly feeling angry about everything.

It's almost like being in adolescence again. And the cosmic joke is that it often hits at a time when our daughters are going through that stage. Let me tell you about a story with my daughter.

We were hugging in the basement car park, after resolving what had become quite a regular argument on the drive home from school. I remember saying "I'm sorry. It's a tricky time for us. We're both going through some big hormonal changes; you at the start of your cycle, and me at the end." It's a cruel thing that menopause usually arrives when you have teenagers going through their own hormonal battles. It was about the only time my teenage son looked like he was truly fascinated by something in his school text book – anything to avoid the explosive emotions coming from this middle-aged woman and her teenage daughter.

I was irritated by her tone; lately she seemed to be always talking to me like I was an idiot. And I was wound up after a day of work where I had reached my limit, being frustrated by the idiocy around me. It struck me that girls and women begin their journey thinking everyone's stupid and enter this last phase feeling the exact same way.

Matt: This is interesting, Susan. I have noticed that some women become a bit less patient.

Susan: Well, let me explain it this way, Matt. There's a myth about women and menopause that's really relevant here.

Matt: I'm listening …

Susan: The myth is that women go crazy during menopause and that we all of a sudden become angry, irrational and resentful. It's a myth! The truth is we are way more likely to show our irritation if you do something that you're not taking accountability for.

Matt: We always seem to get blamed for stuff. How do we fix this?

Susan: By not getting into the fixing!

Matt: Damn, I did it again!

Susan: Let's understand it first. Menopause can cause our emotions to be turbulent, sometimes chaotic. Even though women talk to each other a lot, we don't always have the same experiences during this phase of life, so we have to ride the waves with very little idea where it's all heading. Hot flushes, sweating, mood swings, weight gain, all these things can be confronting and emotionally draining. Depression, anxiety, apathy are all possible symptoms too. So, if we tend to hide our emotions less as we move through midlife and into the second half, I'm not sure you'll get an apology.

The girl who worked so hard to people-please and make herself palatable to the world is starting to give way to a bold-ass woman, and she really does not have the time nor the patience for trivia. Let's be blunt, women generally give less fucks.

- *Someone not listening to you? Their loss!*
- *Being left out of something? Thank God, it was always boring anyway.*
- *There's some gossip around a person you don't like? Not my circus, not my monkeys.*
- *Someone's got an issue with you? That's their problem!*

Matt: Yes, women definitely seem to get more empowered.

Susan: Empowered or just fed up?

A common experience is a loss of patience for the things you used to willingly tolerate. You've suddenly got a voice, and all the resentments you've buried for the last 20 years are surfacing with volcanic force. "I'm not your housemaid. You have 2 capable hands! What did your last slave die from? It's only 1 metre to the dishwasher ... why are your plates in the sink? Why aren't you making your own sandwich ... you are 16 years old!" These little irritabilities come bubbling to the surface to be cleared. We want to make room for the big stuff.

You probably feel more detached about outcomes too. Sometimes you notice you're more fed up than usual, not willing to put up with what you used to tolerate. You realise you actually don't care what other people think anymore, and that so many people around you 'just don't get it'.
Yes, it can look like ...

- *biting a colleague's head off or storming out of a meeting*
- *waking up in the middle of the night wanting to divorce your partner*
- *waking up in the middle of the night and deciding to become a Moulin Rouge dancer*

Matt: That sounds extreme! Why do all these resentments seem to surface out of nowhere? Sometimes I think men aren't equipped to deal with it, and it can come out of the blue.

Susan: Do they really come out of nowhere or are they the issues that have fell on deaf ears for so long? It's true that many feelings of frustration bubble up in the middle stage of life. It's like they have sat dormant in our wombs for half of our lives, then boom, we are suddenly feeling them. Kapow! They come out our mouths with no apparent filter. The clearing is preparing us for the Wise Woman phase. But if you don't work with it productively, it can take you down. There can be so much baggage from things in the past.

If you're a woman, then chances are somewhere along the line you have made a choice to put your own happiness or priorities aside in service to someone else. It's how we're wired. Whether you've taken on the lion's share of the housework, when it should have been equally distributed, or you find your superannuation balance lagging way behind a man's, because you took regular career breaks to have your children, there comes a point when you might reflect: *That's not quite fair.*

Or perhaps you are more than happy with your choices, but when your husband complains he never has any spare time to himself, you hear that inflection in your tone: "Sorry, **you** don't have any time to yourself?"

Maybe it's as simple as having a secret fantasy of floating into Christmas Day with all presents bought and wrapped, house cleaned and decorated, and a banquet prepared for you.

I worked with someone whose wife stopped sleeping with him 10 years ago. He told me it was menopause and that was certainly a plausible explanation. Even Divorce Lawyers are educating themselves on menopause due to the high rates of female-initiated divorces and relationship problems at this time. But it coincidently timed with the aftermath of his affair with his young blonde secretary. "No, we worked through all that. She forgave me," her husband assured me when I gently enquired. "Definitely menopause."

Here's the thing about women: we do what we need to do for that phase of our lives. Sometimes we turn a blind eye because we don't have the energy to face it, sometimes we push it down until a more convenient time, and sometimes hormones mask emotions. In confidence she explained it this way to me: "I just had to keep going; I was raising 3 kids under 4. It's like I didn't even feel it at the time. I was a machine."

Sometimes we carry resentments from a long time back. I once met a lady who was still bitter about her husband leaving her 25 years ago. She spoke about it to anyone who would listen, and had the same fire in her system as if it happened yesterday. He'd moved on and was living a happy life. She was keeping herself stuck in the past. There are many other common female experiences that women keep stored.

Maybe you put your career aside because 'one of us needs to be around for the kids' and guess what, that 'one of us' was you.

Maybe you're having flashbacks of sitting in a meeting room with men dominating the conversation and ignoring your ideas, then raising them as if they were their own.

Or you're remembering that time the sleazy dude from customer service did something highly inappropriate, and you rationalised it at the time with the old adage: 'Boys will be boys.'

For many women, there are themes to our resentments. You might feel particularly angry about:

- *the injustices*
- *the lack of balance in your life*
- *the fact you are always there for people and they aren't there for you*
- *being disrespected, unseen*

Like we said earlier, Matt, our choices or experiences have their way of catching up with us. If not dealt with at the time, emotions get pushed deep down into a dark pit, where they lie ticking like a time bomb waiting to go off. And they tend to explode around midlife.

If you haven't dealt with the emotional debris that's accumulated in your system, chances are it will hit you at menopause. Yes, there are hormones and brain changes that can result in being angry and emotional, but they didn't cause the issue that you now sit with. They are simply amplifying something that's already there and needs to be healed. Unprocessed emotions affect our health. They lie dormant in our systems until they are healed, manifesting themselves as weight, dis-ease, injury and other conditions.

That's why so many people start facing some of these hard issues after a health crisis. There's nothing like a diagnosis to highlight your mortality and see you reflecting on all the things you wished you had, hadn't or 'could have'.

Matt: So, in the end, we all end up in the same place don't we, Susan. Men or women, regardless of our biology or conditioning, if we've buried something rather than faced it at the time, we'd better get ready to deal with it before our second half goes too far.

Susan: Yes, but then we all need to get into the present to cultivate the emotions we really want in our second half. Your process reminds us to practise and strengthen them, by going into those states regularly. Here are some tips I would add for doing this that are targeted at women, but some are relevant to all of us.

Celebrate the positive

We don't do that enough. Make a list now of all the things you are proud of in your life so far. Then remind yourself of them every day.

Develop a routine that works for you

Wild waves of events or emotions are like a rough sea, but the ocean floor is always stable and calm. What keeps you grounded? It might be dance, meditation, yoga, Pilates, listening to mantras, a bath and essential oils. Create a routine so you can go there any time to stabilise or reground yourself.

Make art

Process emotions through your hands – more on that in the next chapter.

Feel to heal

Avoid numbing out or pushing your emotions down. Lock the door, put on some music and feel every inch of them.

Look for the glimmers

Even in rough times, there are moments of beauty, inspiration and bliss. You might just need to look harder for them!

Lean on the sisterhood

In fairy tales, the knight rescues the princess and fulfils her every need. But that's not real life. No 1 person can meet all your needs and support you through everything. It's not

> *fair to ask that of your partner. Here's a tip I feel very lucky to have learnt: take your big emotional issues to your girlfriends! They are qualified for the job, but you need to pick the right friends. Find the queen of your friend circle. She's the one who:*
>
> - *nurtures your inner child*
> - *challenges you in a way that serves your highest good*
> - *helps you find the lesson for you, rather than dragging you into more emotional turbulence*

Matt: Again, those tips are great. My brain is feeling full and blown! And you're absolutely spot on, Susan. What you said about men trying to solve everyone else's problems while dealing with their own internal chaos is dead right. There's something deep within the male psyche that drives this behaviour, and it often comes from the voices of ego and intellect. Those constant, nagging thoughts that create stress and dysfunction. Thoughts like: *I'm better than this guy*, or *Why would you even try that? Have you seen the research?*

Those voices are like a never-ending barrage in a bloke's head, constantly battling to prove someone wrong or meet some impossible expectation, inventing pressure that actually isn't really there. That kind of inner turmoil leads to unhealthy, unhelpful behaviours, towards yourself and others.

The typical way guys tend to deal with it? Denial. Push it down, act like it's not there, and keep moving forward. But does ignoring the problem make it go away? We all know the answer to that is 'no'.

Let me break it down into 'bloke speak'. In fairy tales, the knight slays the dragon and lives happily ever after with the princess. But in real life, those dragons don't just disappear. In fact, they keep showing up fiercer than ever. The scariest dragon? It's the one in your head. The voice that tells you you're not good enough, that you're failing, or that you'll never measure up. That battle is a tough one to win, if you don't have the right tools.

Susan: Do men consider that the best tool is just talking to each other about it? You might see there is common experience.

Matt: I totally get the value of speaking up and finding support, but I've noticed that a lot of groups where men gather to talk about their struggles tend to focus too much on the problem and not the solution. While there's no bad intent in these groups, in my experience, they often end up reinforcing the same struggles. The result? More of the same.

Honestly, I think a lot of men today feel redundant because the 'princess' can slay her own dragons. I have 4 daughters, and I fully support women being empowered to do so. For many men, that shift leaves them feeling lost and unsure of where they fit in or what their purpose is. That's why it's so important for men to have mates who can help them reconnect with themselves in positive ways. These friends help you focus on health, fitness, and those values that really make life worth living.

Let me explain what I've seen work for many men I've coached. In our heads, there's this 'tormentor', who's just like the loud fan in the stands at a sports game who yells at everyone: the ref, the opposition players, even their own team. "Get onside!" "Are you serious, ref?" "He's useless, get him off!" We didn't pay to listen to that person, but they're impossible to ignore. The irony? That loud, obnoxious voice comes from a place of care. If they didn't care, they wouldn't yell.

That's exactly how the voice in your head works. It's constantly nagging you, telling you you're not good enough or that you're failing ... if you let it. Then there's also another voice, a quieter one I like to call the 'Quiet Coach'. It's your internal mentor, and unlike the loud fan, the Quiet Coach doesn't come to you. You have to go to it.

Like all great coaches, your internal mentor answers your questions with more questions: "Why am I feeling this way?" And the coach responds, "Great question. Have you spent some time reflecting on what's going on right now?" The more I ask myself these kinds of questions, the more self-awareness I build, and the better I feel about life. How often do you go to your internal mentor? How well do you know yourself?

Here's what my Quiet Coach has shared with me: 4 simple questions I ask myself every day. They've helped me build a deeper understanding of life, and given me access to a kind of success I never thought I'd experience again:

> **Matt's 4 Simple Questions**
>
> 1. How do you feel? (No lying to yourself – good or bad, it's important to know.)
>
> 2. Why do I feel this way? (Because of the choices I've made, both good and bad.)
>
> 3. How do I want to feel? (I want to feel joy, peace and clarity. How about you?)
>
> 4. What do I need to do to feel that way? (Take action to change the outcome.)

It may seem simple, but spending just 5 minutes each morning and night reflecting on these questions has not only helped me feel better, it's also unlocked a level of success I didn't think was possible anymore. My experience with this is that around 90 percent of the time we actually have the answers to the questions we never ask ourselves. The other 10 percent of the time I suggest to those I'm coaching to seek out external support, like a mentor or clinical support (which worked for me).

Susan: Well said, Matt. And men, we love you and you are so important in our lives, definitely not redundant. Our emotional world would spin completely out of control if you weren't there for us.

Matt: What do you mean?

Susan: I get that the emotions of women can be scary for men. It's a lot to hold, and the temptation is to 'brace for the storm', wait for the cyclone to pass, walk away until we 'can have a civil conversation' or worse still, tell us to 'calm down'. I don't need to tell you that most of the time these strategies don't work, and they usually make it worse.

What we women crave is to have someone witness our emotions, truly hear our concerns and provide some stability that we can't find at the time. Men can be really great at this when it comes to physical safety, but sometimes the emotional field of women can be intimidating. Remember from the second section, feminine versus masculine energy can be compared to things like the moon and sun. Or like a flagpole – the masculine is the sturdy pole that allows the feminine (flag) to dance and move.

So, if I had one tip for men it would be that when she is in an emotional state, lean in. I'm not saying you should allow her abuse or projection; that's a different thing, and boundaries need to be set there. Instead, think about how you can be the stabilising force for her.

Matt: But how do you do that?

Susan: Here's an example for when you are experiencing the heightened emotional state of the opposite sex.

Man: "Okay, tell me what you are feeling at the moment. Talk to me about the emotions you are feeling."

Woman: ...

Man: (Listen like you have never listened before, sit or stand tall in posture, make her see that you are not going to break,

> *bend, walk away or hesitate. Don't try to talk, problem-solve, make it better. Tell her you can handle her emotions ... ask her to express more of her emotions.)*
>
> *Woman: ... (Yep, she'll keep going till she's exhausted.)*
>
> *Man: (Be the flag pole. Do not buckle! Let her know you have understood what she said without trying to jump in, defend, justify or problem-solve. Just paraphrase what you've heard and ask her if you got that right. If it's not glaringly obvious, ask her what she needs from you.)*

Matt: That's a great process, I'm trying that! Any last tips for women?

Susan: I want to encourage everyone to get out there and embrace their emotions. Women, be careful about falling into the conditioning that the world has placed on you. In my generation, the measuring stick has been: 'Be pretty and nice.' We need to show the next generation of women that strong women who work with their emotions are the most powerful force. Let your emotions guide you. Don't feel like you need to 'tone them down' to make everyone else feel comfortable. Speak up about your truths, challenge those around you and set boundaries, all with an open and kind heart. Some people around you won't like it, but they've got some growing to do too!

Matt: And that gives us all something to reflect on. Thank you, Susan.

Section 7

Connection through Spirituality

Chapter 36

Midlife Spiritual Awakenings

"Tell me about your spirituality journey, Matt," Susan enquired politely. Before I could open my mouth, she followed it up with a more mischievous question. "Did a woman get you into it?"

Matt: No, why do you ask?

Susan: That's mostly what I see — women dragging their partners to meditation or a couple's retreat. Then the man usually becomes more committed than the woman! But she usually leads him to it. I think we are more likely to be early adopters of anything woo-woo. We can talk about that more a little later, but first, tell me about your most profound spiritual experience.

Matt: By 2007, I had been meditating for 12 years, having started my spiritual journey after stumbling upon the works of Bruce Lipton and Wayne Dyer. Despite being an atheist at the time, their teachings resonated deeply with me.

After separating from my ex-wife, my eldest daughter and I moved 3 hours away from Canberra, when I took a head coaching job in Sydney. We travelled to Canberra frequently so my daughter could see her mum, and I could spend time with my 3 other daughters. Four years later, I met someone new and we moved in together with her 2 daughters.

One day, as we were heading back to Sydney, my partner's car was packed to the brim with stuff she had picked up from her mum's house in Canberra. Since I had travelled separately a day earlier, I suggested she take my car so the girls would have more space. I picked up my daughter on a stormy night, only to find that she'd had a falling out with her mother. Our drive out of Canberra was tense and quiet, which was unusual for us. We've always been very close.

In my partner's car, we came across an old-style iPod, packed with tunes she used for her job running fashion parade events. My daughter started scrolling through the songs, playing about 10 seconds of each before flicking to the next one. It was driving me crazy. I withdrew into my thoughts, feeling like a victim of a situation that had nothing to do with me.

For some more context, my dad, who passed away when I was 13, had cut a vinyl record in the late 1940s that went to number 2 on Sydney's bestseller list. As we drove towards Lake George, with lightning striking the water's surface, I was so deep in my thoughts that I wasn't appreciating the beauty around me. In that moment, I did something I had never done before or since. I asked myself: *What would you do in this situation, Dad?* Just then, my daughter flicked to the next track, and my dad's song came on. Unbeknown to me, my partner had put it on her iPod along with thousands of other songs.

This overwhelmed me and I started crying, pulling the car over to the side of the highway. "What's wrong, Dad? Are you okay?" my daughter asked. Writing this now, it's still hard to believe. In another person's car, with thousands of songs, I asked an internal question to my dad who had passed away 37 years prior, and bang, his song started playing.

I struggled to speak. My mind was trying to grasp what had just happened, but my heart already knew. I turned to her and whispered, "I asked Dad for help. And then … his song played." She just stared at me. Then, rather than breaking down, we sat there in silence, just listening: *That lucky old sun, had nothing to do, but roll around heaven all day.*

As the crackling vinyl faded into silence, we stared out the windscreen, watching the storm dance across the lake. Cars whizzed past us at 110 kilometres an hour, but we were still, suspended in something bigger than either of us.

I don't know how long we sat there. It could have been minutes, an hour, I have no idea. Eventually, my daughter reached over and placed her hand on my shoulder.

"Dad."

"Yep."

That was it. No more words were needed. I started the car and we drove towards Sydney, the silence between us not empty, but full. Her hand stayed on my shoulder the entire way.

As soon as we arrived home, my perceptive partner asked if I was okay. I explained what happened, and asked if I could sit alone in the dining room for a while. Sitting there, trying to process it all in the dark and quiet room, I internally said: *Okay, Dad, if you're going to show up, let's do it now.* The room went very still, and the atmosphere felt thick. It felt like someone was behind me and about to put a hand on my shoulder. I got scared, opened my eyes, and the room returned to normal.

My partner, again sensing something, came in and asked, "What just happened?"

I replied, "I have no idea what's going on today."

Reflecting on this, and drawing from the understanding of those who work in this area, I believe my dad did show up to support me. He was ready to share his approach to the challenges I was facing, but when he sensed my fear, he withdrew to avoid impacting me negatively.

Since then, I've had similar experiences, and my subconscious fear has made me believe that the good spirits supporting me try to guide me to look within for answers. This has been incredibly helpful, providing great understanding and helping me serve others better.

Susan: That's freaky, Matt, but you're not alone. I can't recall just one experience, but many. I remember lying on the timber floor of my loungeroom looking up at the ceiling: *Is there someone out there? If there is, can you help me ...* The scene took place in my 20s and I was a bundle of nerves and a puddle of tears. It's funny how even non-believers call out to a God in their most desperate times. This was a last resort for me. I had given up trying to get myself out of a relationship mess, and I was hoping that something bigger could save me from my misery and guide me through challenging times.

Later, I was able to see that it was a call to spirituality, but not my first one.

As a young child I loved nature, and you'd often find me gazing deep into the mountains or out to the horizon beyond the sea, filled with awe. I'd feel a sense of wonder at the size of this world and the role 'little me' would play in it all. I was connecting to something bigger, something invisible.

Although it looked very different, that was a call to spirituality too.

In the years approaching my midlife, I began to appreciate the fragility of life. I've always believed age is just a number, but when my calendar struck 50, overnight I seemed to gain more clarity on what was really important. I felt gratitude and a strong desire to give back. I started thinking seriously about the legacy I'd leave. This was a call to spirituality too.

Spirituality has been calling me for as long as I can remember. Sure, the sound of its ring tone has changed throughout the years, and every phase looked different, but they were all a spiritual call.

Chances are this happens to everyone, but it's difficult to know how to label it. After all, there is so much confusion and misunderstanding around the word 'spirituality'.

Matt: Yes, that's the first thing a lot of blokes ask: "What the f*** is spirituality?" You've written a whole book about it, so I'm going to let you take the lead on this one, Susan. The one thing I think we definitely agree on is that spirituality is important.

Susan: I think we agree on a lot more than that. In fact, I think all humans would agree that there is a particular type of feeling that can come over us when we sense a connection to something beyond ourselves. The problem is, if I describe how that feels for me, it's likely that the next person would have a different way of describing it. The difference is not in the human feeling itself, it's in the language we use to describe it, and the rituals we create to generate it and honour it.

Religions have methods to connect like prayer, mantras, meditation, service, singing, whirling, chanting and many more. But spirituality is not the sole preserve of religions.

You don't need to join a group or practise a chant. You don't need to buy crystals or a sage stick. You don't need to be 'gifted', and you don't need to learn some secret language. We all have access to it, anywhere and at any time.

Matt: So, is spiritual practice different for men and women?

Susan: Well, like you, I benefit from meditation. I meditated for nearly 2 decades, and through my daily ritual I established a strong connection to something divine. But things really scaled up when I took a different path. Some of the things that made an even bigger impact for me as a woman included:

- *kundalini dance*
- *bath, oils and body ritual*
- *bodywork and energy massage*
- *kundalini yoga*
- *working with the chakra system in the body*
- *tantra and embodiment work*
- *connecting with cycles, both moon and menstrual*
- *working with women's intuition through card readings*
- *community-based circles with other women*

But I have to say that the biggest turning point was realising that the guru is inside me; it's not something or someone on the outside to be worshipped or followed. The most important practice is to use whatever I need to get into my own body. That's where our spiritual path lies.

I don't believe I'm alone among women in needing to access spirituality through my body. It may be due to our Yin polarity. In the concept of Yin and Yang, men have a yang dominant side, while women have a recessive yin one.

Spirituality is a receptive practice, making it more natural to women.

I notice that men and women access and express spirituality very differently. The thought of meditating in a cave for 3 days may not turn a woman on, but dance, movement, art and nature can be more attractive. And let's be honest, many of the more well-known spiritual practices were designed by men. It is therefore unsurprising that they meet the needs of men, but this is not always true for women.

Matt: Yes, I took to meditation straightaway, but I also find running and moving like mini meditations.

Susan: Let's hear your definition and perspective, Matt. Maybe it will draw in more of the Yang readers.

Matt: When someone asks me to define it, my simple answer is that we are discussing the energy that sits behind everything. Regardless of whether you're an atheist, Christian, Muslim, Buddhist, into quantum physics or tarot cards, there is an understanding that we require energy to exist. I'm not going to expand on where that energy comes from, other than to say this energy is within us and all around us.

As I have mentioned, I like to ask these questions: "Who is thinking your thoughts?" or "Who is experiencing your emotions?" The answer 100 percent of the time is something I spoke about earlier: "I am." This clarifies that you sit behind your brain and nervous system, and that the energy of 'I am' guides how we use our amazing bodies. The goal of focusing on spirituality here is to tap into this 'I am' to improve our lives in the second half. Is that how you would define it, Susan?

Susan: Your explanation makes sense to me, but also proves the point that we will all describe spirituality in our own unique way. Spirituality to me is simply about connection.

From the moment we are born, we leave the safety of our mother's womb and begin our individuation process. We head out into the world to 'find ourselves', and often lose our way. We can only be found in our connection to everything around us. We yearn for connection. I believe everyone feels it, craves it and needs it. The way I think of it is that spirituality is the invisible space that connects us all to everything.

Chapter 37

Spiritual Connection

Matt: I think we become more aware of our spiritual connection as we approach midlife too. Any insights into why?

Susan: The need for this connection often wakes us up during midlife. The spiritual call may start as a subtle nudge, but it will graduate to a loud shout when it's ignored. So, I would encourage our readers not to skip this chapter just because spirituality has not yet been a question you've wanted to explore. Remember, midlife thrusts you into a state of liminality, a bridge between the way you previously structured your identity and your new reality.

During major transitions, our goals, values and sense of self are all in a state of flux. You no longer identify with the status you used to hold, but the new one isn't quite clear yet. I think there are a number of reasons why this happens as we transition to the second half:

- *We may have more time on our hands to contemplate the deeper things in life.*
- *We become acutely aware that there's only one life, and we have a finite opportunity to live it.*
- *We become more grateful for our life, and feel an urge to spread the blessings to others.*

Remember when we talked about 'middlescence', which explained that this transition can be experienced as a state of confusion and disorientation. In my late 40s, I found myself having thoughts like:

- *I don't know if I like what I do anymore, but there's nothing else I want to do. Maybe I need to retire. Or become a florist.*
- *I don't get the same buzz from things that I used to get. Am I depressed? Is there something wrong with me?*
- *I don't care what people think anymore. My sense of self is not coming from anything outside me. I hope I don't turn into a narcissist!*

It's all perfectly normal. You are simply finding yourself again. That can make you feel disconnected for a while, and that's why your spiritual journey beyond midlife is all about connection.

Matt: Okay, Susan. I think you're making a lot of sense out of this confusing topic. I'm a great believer in simple principles. Is there a way you suggest we think about how to find this connection in midlife?

Susan: Well-rounded spirituality involves exploring connection at 3 levels:

1. Connecting with your true self (your spirit, not the egoic identity that may have ruled your first half);
2. Connecting to others;
3. Connecting to a higher force.

Spirituality is an emergent property. If you haven't heard that term before, it means something that is not evident within the individual components of a system, but shows up suddenly when you combine those components. That's why we have moments of heightened spirituality when these 3 levels of connection are in sync. As we connect to something beyond ourselves, we are brought into connection with others, and we naturally focus on improving who we are in the world. Our whole life feels harmonious, and the more we structure our life to prioritise these connections, the more harmonious and spiritual it all feels.

Matt: I find it easy to understand this when I think of the opposite: what it feels like when my life is full of irritation and worries. It's far from harmonious, and those are the times when I feel very far away from my spiritual centredness.

I think we should spend time exploring these 3 levels a bit more.

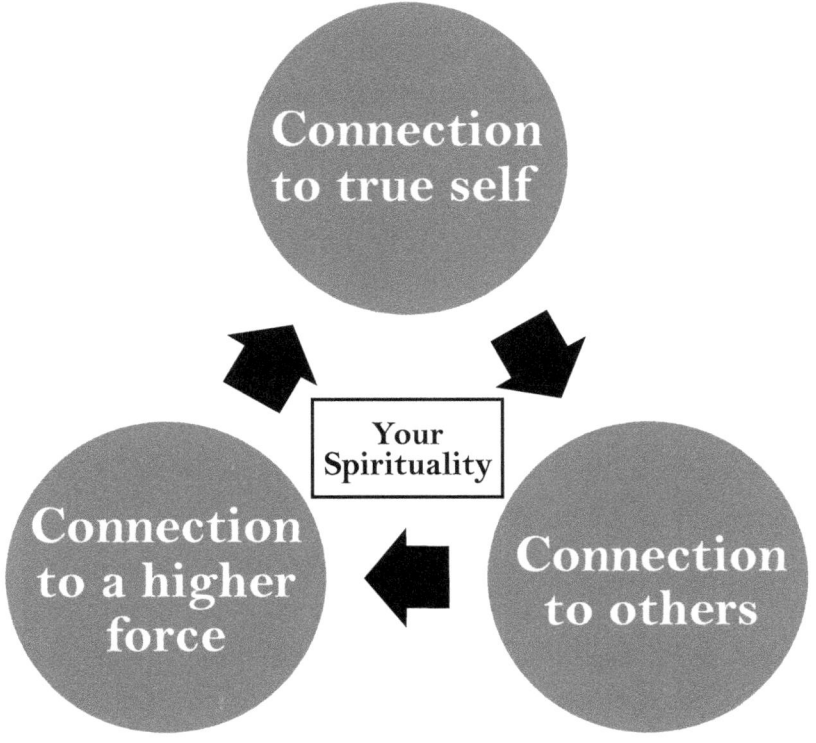

Chapter 38

Connecting with Your True Self

The prizes for the first half of life are for 'achievement', not for 'personality'.

Carl Jung, Swiss psychiatrist and psychoanalyst

Susan: 'Your true self' is a big concept and sometimes something tricky to define. Sitting at the half way point of your life, how do you assess whether you've 'done well'? If you're really honest, I bet your mind drifts to your bank account, house, car and other things you own. Maybe the number of overseas trips you've taken, your place on the career ladder, salary and debt, or lack thereof. You probably also think about the children you've raised and the people you've mentored, guided and helped.

But the reality is, many of us spend the first half of our lives simply accumulating things. After all, we're bombarded with the messages that happiness, arguably life's ultimate goal, comes from external sources. Even when we know this is not true, it's very hard to resist those pressures.

The second half presents an opportunity to get to know your real self, the self who would still be present without the possessions, status, labels and other trappings. We could define this as your spirit, the never-changing part of you that has been there since the day you were born.

You're so much more than your body, yet at middle age it's easy to become preoccupied with stiff joints, ageing skin, high cholesterol and a growing mid-section. The fact that many people remain in the builder phase of their life well into their second half can also create a clash of priorities. It's hard to get to know your 'spirit' when the body it's housed in feels like a broken vessel. Or you're worried about your bank balance, so addressing all those issues is super important, but so too is nurturing your internal system.

Matt: In my language, you're talking about how I tap into my 'I Am'. In life, we develop so much expertise in the work that we do, the places we go, the hobbies we enjoy, the children we raise, the cars we drive and a myriad of external interests, but how much expertise do we develop in ourselves? How often do you take the time to sit down and study yourself? The most consistent answer I get to this question is: "Never."

I often struggle with the arm wrestle between my Old Self and Best Self. As a white Australian male on my 60th lap around the sun, I have many entrenched belief systems and subconscious behaviours that do not support the growth I want to achieve, and the impact I want to make in the second half. As someone who has been meditating for 30 years, I have often come out of practices with complete clarity on how I can be better, only to end up at the pub later in the day criticising someone behind their back for something completely inane. I know I'm not alone in this habit, which seems to have become completely normalised in our modern era.

Once you begin increasing your understanding of yourself, you'll not only see the incredible unique abilities you bring to the planet, but you'll also have to confront the unhelpful and destructive behaviours that are ingrained into your life. Like so many things that are worth doing, the good news can also bring tough news, and your ego will show up unannounced quite often in this journey.

Susan: This is true of all change, but the beauty of midlife is that we have many motivations to take this journey, and many comrades beside us on the same road. We can lean on each other and listen to other people's stories, to help us find what will work well in our unique life.

Matt: So true, Susan, and the elements we've talked about in the other chapters all weave together on this spiritual adventure:

- *You will experience spiritual heights through great physical energy.*
- *Quietening your mental activity with mindfulness and meditation provides space to connect with your real self.*
- *Negative emotions give you hints to your wounds, and to where your healing opportunities lie. Positive emotions elevate you to a whole and connected state.*

Okay, Susan, I'm on board. Self-awareness is one of my favourite topics and we spoke about it in our chat about mind training too. How do I connect with my true self?

Susan: Here are some other ideas.

Reflection

We all do this in different ways. I do this in nature swims or walks, my mum does it through quiet contemplation at church, my dad achieves it when fishing, my friend does it during regular energy massages, and my mate does it by going on regular camping weekends, deep in the wilderness by himself.

It can look different for everyone, but the premise is the same: find time in your life to reflect on how you want to live, and whether you are in alignment to those desires. It's also a time where you can start to feel that part of you that is stable and unchanging, when you fall still and without the noise of the busy mind.

Questions are the key to prompting deep reflection. It's not that everyone avoids self-awareness in their first half, but generally a different set of questions emerge as we move through the transition from first to second half.

Use the questions below to journal your reflections and see what emerges.

FROM (common first half questions)	*TO* (common second half questions)
What do I want to achieve?	How do I want to feel?
What do I have to do?	What do I stand for?
What does everyone else want from me?	What do I want, desire and need in my life?
What are my qualifications?	What are my strengths and values?
Am I successful?	What am I grateful for?
Am I better or worse than others?	Who is the unique me?
Who or what is standing in the way of what I want?	What are the self-imposed obstacles I'm allowing to impact on my desires? How can I work on those?
Where am I failing?	What principles do I want to guide my life?

Matt: I can't reinforce enough how powerful it can be to ask yourself questions like these. Even if you think you've asked them before, it's surprising how the answers change at different points in your life.

So, Susan, imagine you're starting to get some of these answers; what's next then?

Use Joy to Love Yourself Up!

Susan: You're rolling your eyes, I know. It sounds so cliché, and I probably would have been cynical about the phrase too, until I did it. If you've spent a lifetime giving to everyone else, or you're the type of person who works really hard to get love from others, your life changes exponentially when you invest in giving yourself the love you crave.

Don't wait anymore. Indulge in joyful pleasures that you might normally plan for someone else, or that you have been going without because you wished someone else would plan them for you. Allow yourself to have the life, relationships and world you deserve. Invest in yourself every single day, week, month and year.

> *Brainstorm a list of all the things that bring you great joy, and start bringing them into your life. Consider these:*
>
> - *massage*
> - *flowers or pieces of art in your home*
> - *a slow Sunday cook-up*
> - *personal development course*

- *exotic holiday*
- *dancing*
- *swimming in the ocean*
- *essential oils in the bath*

Matt: Okay, Susan, now you've explained it, I can see why it's so important to do this intentionally. Sometimes it can be difficult to believe we deserve this joy and love, and if you're a 'giver', it's even harder to put yourself first. But we need to believe in our own worthiness.

Susan: I'm glad to hear you say that, Matt. If we don't believe we deserve to be honoured, how can our bodies trust it's safe to reveal some of the answers on our spiritual path? Of course, loving yourself up also means owning and accepting every single part of you, for better or for worse, so here's something else to try.

Speak kindly to yourself

When your internal voice speaks to you in terms that are critical, negative or insulting in any way, put the voice on pause for a moment. Think of kind things to say to yourself, as if you were encouraging a friend or child to accept themselves and love themselves just the way they are.

Practise speaking kindly to yourself whenever it comes to mind.

Matt: Susan, remember when you asked me who I would invite to dinner, back at the start of the book? I just experienced a lightbulb moment as you explained your last tip. I'm going to say there is no-one I would want at dinner more than my 10-year-old self. He was a kid who would lay on his back in the backyard, staring at the night sky, wondering what was beyond the furthest star he could see. If there was a wall around the universe, he'd wonder what was outside of that.

This kid valued connecting with people over education, recognition or money. He saw the goodness in everyone and had no time for negativity. His energy was focused on fun, adventure, and playing sport with friends. Of course, that focus didn't always lead to the best school marks, and probably resulted in a few too many trips to hospital for stitches or a plaster cast.

If I got the chance to chat with him now at dinner, I'd wait for the sticky date pudding, and this is what I'd say:

> "Mate, in the future, a lot of people will try to guide you down certain paths to fit their version of success. It will be really tough not to become addicted to external validation. There will be times when it feels easier to lie rather than tell the truth, just to avoid hurting others' feelings or being judged.
>
> Your circle of friends will shrink as you put more attention into family and career but trust me, the good ones always stick around. Most importantly, understand that challenges in life are inevitable. You can either take them personally or see them as opportunities for growth.

The key message? Matthew, never stop living from the goodness within you. You already have all the wisdom you'll ever need. You have the energy to do everything you want. And if you love life, your passions won't turn into work that damages your relationships and health."

What I've learnt since becoming a granddad is that we need to learn from kids more than they need to learn from us. They live fully in the moment. We restrict ourselves too much, worrying about imagined threats, getting angry about things happening on the other side of the planet, or stressing about how we're going to get paid. And that stress? It's the biggest cause of disease and death on the planet.

So, why do we do this to ourselves? That's the answer my 10-year-old self needed to hear, to persuade him to keep living exactly as he was.

Susan: And 60-year-old Matt, what's stopping you from doing it now?

Matt: It's time.

Susan: Well, maybe the next tip can help.

Ritual as Reminder

Susan: Even when we have good intentions of connecting with our spirituality, in this fast-paced world it's easy to forget that side of yourself as you're sipping your first morning coffee. Rituals can act as reminders.

Every day, shortly after I wake up, I sit on a mat and I ask myself: *What do I need today?* Sometimes I close my eyes for 10 seconds and get straight off the mat. But other times, I do 40 minutes of yoga or 20 minutes of meditation.

This plug-in, no matter how long I invest, changes my day. I wonder if that's where prayer originates? At school, I was taught a morning prayer and a night-time prayer. I realise now they can anchor your day and remind you there's something other than the external chaos of life.

> *What helps you fall still and connect with your true self? It might be:*
>
> - *reading a page of an uplifting book*
> - *lighting a candle*
> - *listening to a song that connects you*
> - *putting your face up to the sun*
> - *breathwork*

The options are limited only by your imagination.

Identify the times within your day where your new ritual could fit. Experiment with those times until you build some momentum. Don't give up too early. New habits require some repetition before they stick.

Matt: I've got an example of something I do that combines a few of the suggestions in your tips. When I want to create new constructive behaviours and leave redundant ones behind, I set myself a target and I journal my progress. For example, if I want to stop saying things about people when they are not around (because let's face it, that sort of comment is usually pretty judgemental or negative), I make an agreement with myself to only share my feedback with the person it is directed towards. Then I keep score for 6 weeks to see how often I break the agreement. Zero is my move-on mark.

I have used this approach with things like self-confidence, installing new habits, and feeling the presence of my 'I Am' all day.

Susan: That's a really well-designed approach, Matt. Your 10-year-old self would be very proud of you!

Chapter 39

Connecting to Others

Matt: Okay, what about connecting to others? This is such an important area. My family and my mates are everything to me. Plus, there is so much research saying that relationships are the key to longevity.

Susan: Even in our own survey, both men and women ranked family as their number one priority to midlife and beyond. Let's broaden the definition of family for a moment, while I tell you a story.

Picture this: every morning, as the sun begins to peek above the horizon, a group of men gather by the shore, sharing tales and laughter. Eventually they peel off their jackets and approach the waves, slowly submerging themselves in the ocean. Some swim skilfully out past the breakers, others feel more comfortable bouncing around where their feet can still touch the sand. They've been doing this for nearly 30 years, ever since a few of them retired to this beachside town. Their average age is around 85, and their membership has ebbed and flowed as new friends join, and old mates pass away.

I have always been inspired by 'The Pod'. These men (and the occasional woman) are the epitome of good health. Their bodies may have changed, but the joy they feel during their daily swim and connection with each other remains constant. Some of this can be attributed to exercise and the replenishing nature of Vitamin Sea. But the 'power of the pod' cannot be underestimated. When you surround yourself with people who are joyous, healthy and wise, you are swept into the rip of vitality. Simply knowing you belong to such a group, boosts your wellbeing, spirituality and happiness.

Matt: I couldn't agree more. I have a very similar group called 'The Plungers'; we either have a morning ice bath or jump in the ocean in the middle of winter. What about you? Have you got a social support network?

Susan: I have a few different types. I have one friend who consistently calls on a Monday to see what my week holds, and then again at the end of the week to check on how it unfolded. Sometimes I find myself feeling bothered, because I tell myself I don't have time for the 10-minute call, especially when I'm juggling school drop-off and getting ready for work. But it turns out this lovely friend is partly responsible for my positive state of wellbeing. A *New York Times* article, published on the 1 January 2023, reported that having someone hold space for you for merely 8 minutes, a couple of times a week, can significantly reduce depression and anxiety, and boost overall wellbeing.

Matt: I think most of us realise relationships are important, but they might be even more important than you think. Numerous studies over the years have found that people with healthy relationships are happier, live longer and have less health problems. Now there's a prescription worth paying attention to! Your life literally depends on the degree to which you can relate to others.

Here's a few interesting research findings I came across:[12]

- *Poor social relationships will increase a person's risk of premature death. This rivals smoking, obesity and lack of physical exercise.*
- *Social isolation was associated with a 29 percent increased risk of heart disease, a 32 percent increased risk of stroke, and a 50 percent increased risk of dementia.*
- *Loneliness was associated with higher rates of depression, anxiety and suicide.*

And this one's interesting:

- *Loneliness among heart failure patients was associated with nearly 4 times increased risk of death, 68 percent increased risk of hospitalisation, and 57 percent increased risk of emergency department visits.*

We're talking public health and longevity, not necessarily spirituality, but these stats really make you stop and pay attention.

Susan: Social isolation (or a lack of social connections) is the biggest risk factor facing ageing people today, and it seems like people are really feeling it. While we are nerding out on research, I also found the US study referred to on the previous page. It showed that more than one third of adults aged 45 and older feel lonely, and nearly one quarter of adults aged 65 and older consider themselves socially isolated.

COVID, and its consequent periods of forced isolation, played a role in creating a 'new norm'. I have watched myself decline more invitations, because comfort is now found in the

---

12 - See References 12.

home. This can be amplified at midlife because it's often the 'empty nest' phase, when children move on and all the social interactions instigated through them (think school functions, sport activities) drop away.

But I like to ask, is the 'empty nest' phase not an opportunity? As you're rattling around with all that extra space and time, how are you going to fill it? After all, our brains are wired to be social, to live in community with others and help each other out. There's a reason why practising spirituality, religious or not, isn't a solo job.

- ✓ We learn more in community.
- ✓ We heal faster in community.
- ✓ Wisdom is shared more easily in community.
- ✓ Communities hold us accountable.
- ✓ Communities keep us safe through the hard times.
- ✓ Communities give us a buzz, by showing us firsthand that the sum is always greater than its parts.
- ✓ Communities remind us that we are never alone.

Matt: And there is nothing that will reveal more of your areas for self-development than your relationships with others! It's like a mirror. So, what type of community do you suggest people need to surround themselves with?

Susan: It's largely a personal choice, but here are my suggestions for making the connections that work for you.

Tip 1: Find Your Tribe

Your tribe is the group where you feel safe, supported and encouraged to be yourself. You learn, grow and are challenged there. You can ask for help and you offer help freely.

Your tribe probably think in similar ways to you (on the big stuff anyway) and hold similar values to you. At the same time, it's good if they challenge you with different opinions and diverse thought too!

The tribe you had when you were young is not necessarily the same one you need now. It's important that your tribe views midlife similarly to the way you do.

People usually go one of 2 ways as they age:

1. Some get old, grumpy, resistant to change and set in their ways. You can see this on their faces, and they literally look 20 years older than their peers.

2. Others see themselves on a new and exciting adventure. They have so much left in their tank to give, and they are going to give their all.

Which group do you surround yourself with? It's an important question, because you become the average of the 5 people you spend most time with. Now I'm not suggesting you do a friend and family cull, but it's a useful reflection. Who shares the same philosophy, outlook, values and enthusiasm?

> *If suitable people don't come to mind, find a new tribe. Start doing more of what you love, and you'll soon meet people who love it too. Join a club, do a course, go to a social event and find them. You may end up with many different tribes for different purposes.*
>
> *Personally, I have:*
> - *Friends who will listen to my challenges and help me to elevate my thinking, take responsibility and find resolutions, not suck me deeper into the drama.*
> - *Women I can 'let loose' with, and share great joy.*
> - *Friends with whom I share lifetime memories and can trust to have my back.*
> - *Friends with common interests – this group can change regularly.*
>
> *Where will you find your tribe?*

Matt: I've been lucky enough to be part of teams since I was young, and I feel like this has made me really aware of the importance of having connections with people who love what I love. As we've all grown older, many of us evolved into new interests, but it's probably unsurprising that health and fitness still rank high for a large proportion of my friendship groups. In fact, many of my connections are deeper in the second half, because we all appreciate how important our shared priorities are.

Okay, what's the next tip?

> ## Tip 2: Clean Up Your Intimate Relationships
>
> *The quality of your intimate relationships is very important. A study found that women in their midlife, who were in highly satisfying marriages, had a lower risk of cardiovascular disease compared with those in less satisfying marriages.*
>
> *But we also know that arriving into midlife with more time on your hands can mean getting to know your partner all over again. This won't always be pretty! There may be some edges or boundaries to renegotiate.*
>
> *It's easy to grow complacent, so find ways to connect again through a joint hobby or pursuit. Spend time really listening to each other, and seeing each other as a new person entering a new phase. Talk about your needs in this phase of your life. Have fun together and laugh like you used to. This is a very important time to invest in each other.*

Matt: As someone without a long-term partner, the opportunity to form a new intimate relationship is something I hope comes my way. I learnt a lot of lessons from my past relationships, the most important of which was self-awareness. That's why I believe relationships really are spiritual work.

Susan: So true, Matt. It was only years after my marriage ended that I was able to see my own patterns in those relationships. Maybe one day both of us will be in relationships where we can do our spiritual work with a like-minded partner in real time. In the meantime, there are plenty of other opportunities to connect with people in our communities.

> ## Tip 3: Create Community
>
> *I have a good friend who is a powerhouse businesswoman, but in midlife she decided to dial that down and spend her time volunteering for a local thrift shop. Her passion for fashion grew, and she found an outlet for her creative expression by styling outfits. It even took her to the runway of Fashion Week. But above all, she simply loved giving back to the community.*
>
> *She joins the increasing number of people choosing to volunteer their time and energy to community causes later in life. Why? Because it feels good! The benefits to the 'giver' are often greater than those to the 'receiver'. We are designed to help each other out.*
>
> *Volunteering rates have increased significantly over the last decade, because people recognise the joy it brings and the difference it makes. You can decide to commit to something long term, or put your hand up for the occasional need, such as helping with recovery efforts or in crisis situations.*

There are many other ways to connect to your community:
- *Participate in a park run or a local community exercise club.*
- *Join a club and help with fundraising.*
- *Go to community events.*
- *Help with a community garden.*
- *Hangout regularly at your local coffee shop and get to know other locals.*
- *Go to a rally.*

Get involved in anything that gives you a sense of belonging to a group. After all, belonging is critical to our wellbeing!

Matt: Love those ideas.

Chapter 40

Connecting to a Higher Force

Now things were getting interesting. I had the feeling we were about to go all woo-woo, and I was up for it! But I also recognised that not everyone would be comfortable going there.

Matt: Before you talk about the third level, I want to address something I think a lot of blokes out there will be questioning: "What are the benefits?". If you can't draw a line between meditating for an hour a day, volunteering or going to a place of worship and experiencing a better life, maybe you'll relate to the practical benefits of spirituality.

Susan: Fair point. And in reality, many people take on some of these practices for practical benefits, only realising the deeper impact many years down the track.

Matt: Here are some reasons for people to take the leap into this stuff:

- **Enhanced mental clarity**: *Regular spiritual practices can clear mental clutter, making you more focused and decisive in daily tasks.*
- **Emotional resilience**: *Understanding and connecting with your 'I Am' helps in managing stress and emotions, leading to a more balanced and harmonious life.*

- **Improved relationships**: *As you become more self-aware and centred, your interactions with others become more genuine and compassionate, fostering stronger and healthier relationships.*
- **Physical health**: *There is ample evidence suggesting that spiritual practices can lower blood pressure, improve sleep, and boost overall physical health.*

In essence, accessing spirituality equips you with tools to handle life's challenges more effectively, enhancing your quality of life in the second half. Integrating spiritual practices into your daily life can elevate your wellbeing and accelerate your recovery. Enhancing connection to your inner energy also benefits those with whom you share your life.

Susan: I agree with all those benefits. It has literally changed my life. One of the reasons that belonging to a group and connecting to others lights up our brain is because it takes us away from our human tendency to obsess about ourselves. But nothing's better than contributing to something that's way bigger.

We all come at this from our own unique place, and we all have different desires and tolerances when it comes to practising spirituality. So, I'm going to look at this in a few different ways – think of it like a 'choose your adventure' approach. You could:

- *Dive in; or*
- *Test the waters; or*
- *Dip your toe in.*

Matt: I love a good adventure!

Susan: You and I are definitely 'dive in' types. Hopefully many readers are too, so here's what that might look like.

Dive in: Connect to Something Beyond

Is there something 'bigger' out there? We personally think so, but even if it turns out to be a false prophecy, the belief is definitely not doing any harm. Study after study reveals that people with a higher faith in a force that connects and guides us, tend to be happier than those who don't.[13] For some people, this belief comes in the form of religion and an associated 'God' figure. Others find it through a yogic tradition, complete with a guru and set of doctrines or practices.

Some people believe it's all pure science. Quantum physics talks about an invisible field with a unifying principle that binds everything together. Matt, you've spoken a lot about energy, and every single thing with energy vibrates, including us. For example, there is ample evidence that your brain vibrates at different frequencies, depending on your state. Scientists can record gamma waves when you are learning, delta waves when you sleep, and theta waves when you are in deep meditation.

You can influence your frequency, but that works both ways. Stress generates frequencies that make you feel worse; positive actions, such as the things we've spoken about in this book, will shift your frequency in ways that feel uplifting.

You don't have to sign up to any of those ideologies. I've enjoyed adopting practices from many traditions and beliefs, and I'm not sure which school of thought I belong to; but I definitely can't deny all the events in my life that have shown

---

13 - See References 13.

me something bigger at play. It's like the story with your dad, Matt. Everyone has probably had an experience where they've:

- *met people in their life they knew they were meant to meet. It may be a partner or a friend who has changed your life. It probably felt like 'destiny', or that someone was watching and somehow controlling the puppet strings.*
- *had an 'event' delivered to them which was devastating at the time, but when they look back, they realise it offered a learning they needed to receive.*
- *felt like they were put on a path to something great, and were delivered to where they really needed to be.*

Maybe you've heard one of those weird stories of someone's experience with a psychic, tarot card reader, ouija board, past-life or near-death experience that was too unbelievable to be fake. Some people call this higher force God; some call it 'destiny', 'the universe', 'the quantum field' – the label doesn't matter. If you feel like you've connected to a force that's bigger than you, or you really want to, here are some tips for diving into a deeper connection with a higher force.

Talk to it

Spiritual guidance can only come to you if you have open lines of communication. Religious traditions have prayer, and some spiritual traditions set intentions around specific moon phases. Those working with the quantum field attend closely to their thoughts and words, conscious of the impact these have on energy.

Find your way to tell the universe or your higher force what you want. Ask for support during challenging times, give your problems over to this force and give gratitude back to it. Then listen and look for signs and guidance.

Have faith

When you truly believe there's a force supporting you and helping you to grow, your perspective on events changes. When something negative happens to me now, I no longer pre-occupy myself with how bad the other person's actions were, or any perceived unfairness. Instead, I reset my boundaries, then focus more of my time thinking about questions like:

- *What did I learn from this?*
- *How do I want to grow?*
- *What emotion needs to be processed here? How can I support myself to do that?*

Matt: That's one of the golden questions isn't it: "What did I learn?" I try to remember to ask this question every day!

Test the Waters: Connect to Nature, Art, Music

Susan: Okay, if you're not quite ready for all the woo-woo, don't worry, you can still experiment with connecting to a higher force. There's one with us every day: nature.

I love all forms of being in nature – hiking in the rainforest, looking out to a mountain view, sitting around a fire – but if I had to choose, my favourite is definitely the ocean. When I swim in the ocean, I seek out calm waters where I can lay back and float. I am awed by how she seems to be holding me; I feel so connected to every single drop. I can look all around and never really comprehend her vastness. It really does make me feel relaxed, held, connected, still, blissful.

The good thing about nature is that you never have to make sure she's got time for you. She's always there. I go to the ocean when I need healing. Maybe I've had a busy week/month/year. Sometimes I've been through something sad that I need washed away from me, and she does that. There's no-one else, just me and her. All her invisible properties and her energy weaves with mine, creating magic. Nature is a great place to start a spiritual journey, and it's right at your doorstep.

Again, if you like to keep some science in your approach, there are many studies confirming that being in nature improves overall wellbeing. I'm sure you've felt that shift in your state, dare I say it, a change in your frequency of vibration.

What's your favourite experience in nature, Matt?

Matt: I shared my story about regularly paddling around the Sydney waterways with my friend. Our connection with nature is a priority on those mornings, and I definitely feel my body relax and move into a different energy state. For me, it's physical, mental, emotional and spiritual. I feel deeply connected to everything after those experiences.

Susan: There is something deeply spiritual about art too. One of my second-half clients had an awakening (that's probably the positive way of looking at it) and emerged as a hugely talented artist. He had never picked up a paintbrush in his life, and all of a sudden, he was producing masterpieces. It's not the first time I've witnessed that. In some way, the creation of art helps people to connect to a higher force, and they simply become the instrument for divine creation. Now, this is not a personal experience I've had when painting. The quality of my art hasn't improved since high school, but I have no doubt the practice can become a spiritual meditation.

There are plenty of other forms of art to try – dancing, writing, pottery, singing, or anything that brings out your deep and divine creative expression. The one for you is probably the one you have buried for a long time, just like I did with drumming!

Music is another spiritual doorway. I've shared the story of how I learnt the drums when I turned 50. It wasn't just about learning an instrument. Music has pulsated in my veins since I was born. At 50, it was time to let it come out. The 'high' I receive from expressing myself musically can't be described. Even when I started out, it was like riding a wave of grace. When I had the opportunity to jam with someone else, I got to see firsthand how the whole was much bigger than the sum of its parts. I felt so connected, out of my head and in my body. It felt like everything I've always felt spirituality to be. The drums have led me into more spiritual places, and

I brought percussion into my work – bongos and shakers became my healing instruments.

Do you have a budding rock guitarist, DJ, lead singer or harp player wanting to come out in you? Now is the time.

Connect to nature

Find your favourite piece of nature and go there regularly.

Don't just walk straight through her, really connect. Pay more attention to the visual delight around you than to the million thoughts in your head. Communicate with her (listen, smell, touch, breath it all in) and see what feelings arise.

Explore art and music

Use your hands to find your creative spiritual expression.

If you're not sure what it is, enjoy experimenting with many options until you find the one that feels like it comes from deep inside you.

Dip Your Toe In: Find Your Purpose

Susan: If that is still too much for you, don't worry; there's another option you can try: uncover and live your purpose.

Our priorities naturally shift to service in midlife. I've noticed that "What would I do if I won the lottery?"

answers at a dinner party start to become more serious, more meaningful. On the surface, this may not make sense. Surely, you'd use the $30 million to fund your new yacht, complete with captain and cook, or beach houses on every continent, and plenty of new cars, of course. But when most people are pushed to consider a life with no limits, it usually involves giving back in some way.

At this stage of life, we now understand that money doesn't buy happiness. Researchers studied lottery winners and found that, while there was initial excitement, within just 12 months their happiness levels returned to the same point they were prior to the win.[14] Neuroscientists will tell you that the brain's reward centres light up in huge ways when people are making a difference, giving back and being purposeful. In fact, they light up more than chocolate, money or sex!

Matt: So, is there a way you can work out your purpose? I feel like I found mine in coaching people in wellbeing and performance. In some ways it wasn't found, because it was always there, just in different forms.

Susan: *You can never connect the dots until you're looking back.* This was a line from a famous speech by the late Steve Jobs to an audience of college graduates. When I heard this, it struck a chord. In the first couple of phases of your life, you often make decisions based on intuition, opportunity, grace and ease. Sometimes they don't even make sense to you, or have any logical explanation, but when you look back, you can see they have paved a neat path to your future destiny.

Many people switch careers in their second half of life. Even if you're not looking for a career, chances are you'll

---

14 - See References 14.

have a second bloom; seeds lie dormant waiting to sprout. "I'd like to do more travel. I'd love to write a travel blog just for the fun of it," my sister once shared on a morning walk.

Matt: We all have gifts, and we were all put on the earth for a reason. You may have used these gifts to earn money, support your family, or for your own gain. In the second half of life, you are likely to experience a yearning to offer these gifts to the world.

Susan: For women in particular, the second half is often when you can finally explore the things you've always wanted to do. The kids are gone and there's time, but you might question what you have to offer, or lack the confidence to really go for it.

Matt: Yes, I think confidence is an issue for both sexes. I've had to work on it and also learn to sit with the discomfort of venturing into the uncertainty of something new. It would have been easier for me to stick with the industry I knew and spent my whole life in. But exploring new horizons is always worth it. Have you got any tips for building up confidence?

Susan: I say, take a fresh look at yourself. We often discount skills gained outside the workplace. When we submit a job application, it doesn't ask us for the negotiation skills gained through our divorce, or the leadership skills it requires to get 4 people sitting down at the dinner table at the same time. It doesn't leave scope for us to highlight the relationship building skills we learnt at Friday afternoon drinks, or the tough communication skills learnt when navigating a dispute in your close-knit friendship group. You gather new skills, experiences and attributes every moment of your life, whether it's in a workplace, at home, on a stage or at the school tuckshop.

Matt: Very true. My advice is if you feel a calling towards something with greater purpose and meaning, do it. A life of service will give you a deep sense of reward, and that's a spiritual life. For someone just getting started with this, what do you suggest?

Uncover your purpose by asking yourself these questions:

- **What are my strengths?** *What are those broad, fundamental characteristics and attributes that you bring to every situation, whether it's a work team, social group, sporting team or to your friends and family. Take some time to reflect on this. Chances are you've spent a lot of time reflecting on your weaknesses, so turning your attention to strengths may feel challenging. Ask friends, family members, colleagues and those closest to you. They can often see the wonderful things you can't see in yourself.*

- **What am I passionate about?** *Think about the times you really feel like you're making a difference. What is it that really lights you up?*

- **How can I use my strengths and my passions in service to the world?** *Identify the small things you can start doing right now to use your strengths and spend time on your passions. Also dream about the big steps that can turn your purpose into the main act in your life. As soon as you get moving on this path, you'll be amazed how it unfolds before you.*

Matt: You've got so much to give with all your acquired wisdom by the time you reach the second half. In areas of the planet called 'Blue Zones', which have the highest concentration of healthy people over 100 years of age, the older people are, the more they are sought out to provide the deepest insights on life. They not only provide their communities with amazing access to spiritual wisdom; it also gives their lives greater purpose. This translates into improved personal wellbeing.

In many cultures, like indigenous people in Australia, elders' knowledge is respected and revered. Sharing this wisdom benefits the giver and receiver. But in modern life, most of us are exposed to a false redundancy mindset, suggesting that when you reach a certain age, the contribution you can make to personal and professional environments reduces. This loss of purpose and meaning sees people retreat back into themselves. They only get asked about their history, and not what they can share now that will improve lives. Ultimately, we put elderly people into homes where many rarely see family, and all meaning in life slowly dissolves, along with their wellbeing.

The challenge for men in the second half is that these conversations are difficult to ignite, because our conditioning says this stuff is 'out there'. This results in us confining everything inside, or waiting for when the shit really hits the fan, when we are in real turmoil.

The more you take time to understand your own energy, the more you can help others tap into their spiritual development. What I have found in most cases is that all you need to do is be prepared to start the conversation, then most blokes are more than happy to join in. Very few don't engage; they either don't need it to feel content, or they just aren't ready yet.

Spirit doesn't give a shit how old you are. There are many people who have accessed a high level of spiritual wisdom and they have so much to share that we can learn from. So, regardless of who you are or how old you are, make sure you utilise the most important spiritual tool of listening.

I've started talking about men here, but we can't end without answering the question: "Do you think women are better at spirituality than men?"

Susan: Ha-ha, no, I wouldn't say that. At the spirit level, I believe we are all the same. The spirit doesn't have a gender or personality, but comes from the same source. However, I am going to return to science for a few interesting facts. We briefly explored the link between spirituality, energy and frequency. Now consider some of these findings.[15]

- *Brain scientists have discovered that frequency comes from grey matter. Women have more brain cells in their grey matter than men, which might indicate they have greater potential for affecting the world around them with their frequency. In addition, it's been suggested that women are more sensitive to frequency. It's what we've labelled to date as 'women's intuition', and most women can relate to the ability to tap into information that can't be seen by the eye.*
- *Big generalisation, but it's been suggested that women may naturally be able to connect with the universe better than men. This is because the universe is made up of*

---

15 - See References 15.

atoms and electrons that make protons and neutrons, similar to cells that make up our body structure. Women have more protons and neutrons in their body structure, which may allow them to exchange energy better with the universe. It's an interesting one, because you'll remember in the feminine and masculine polarity discussion, one of women's greatest strengths is to bring energy.

Matt: That blows my mind, but also makes sense. I think for both sexes it's remembering that our spirits don't age. We accumulate wisdom through understanding the energy behind life. This helps us understand ourselves and others who share this planet, and it also helps us to connect with the meaning behind our existence. As humans, the main process for accumulating wisdom has been by experiencing life. We learn through the contrast of getting things right, and fucking things up.

When it comes to building self-awareness, I think it's worth mentioning that finding the process that works isn't a static thing. I don't think I've met anyone who would say, "Yep, I've meditated for a year and I fully understand myself and where life is taking me. Now I can put the cue back in the rack!"

To attain great results and maintain the benefits, you need to consistently and systematically stick to the practice. Just like exercising or learning, you don't just do it once and have it covered for life. If you stop, the benefits slowly wane, and the reality is that these capacities become redundant if you don't restart the process.

If you're worried about being able to maintain your enthusiasm for repeating the same activities day after day, here's the fun side: many different methods can tap into your core energy, and it is sometimes beneficial to stimulate your mind with new activities to spark new pathways to knowledge.

Susan: Variety is the spice of life, and there's no doubt that every one of us has our own unique path to spirituality.

Section 8

Embracing the Full-Time Hooter

Final Words for Now

I had a feeling we could talk for 5 more years about winning the game in the second half of life. It filled me with a touch of sadness to feel our conversations, at least in this round, were coming to an end.

Susan: We've talked about a lot in this book, Matt.

Matt: We sure have, and there are at least 100 tips that people can try.

Susan: Which kind of makes it all sound like hard work, considering our message is to enjoy the second half!

Matt: That reminds me of a chat I had with my old mate, Reg. He came to me one day saying a penny had dropped. "We're 59, Matt. That means we've got 24 years to go according to the stats, so I reckon we need to start enjoying ourselves."

I sighed, just a bit. "First, Reg, I don't give a damn about stats. Second, you and I have packed enough fun into our lives for 10 lifetimes. And third, you've never followed the rules, so why start now?"

Reg was persistent. "Mate, we've got to deal with the realities of life and make sure we enjoy ourselves."

"I agree, brother," I said, "but how about we just focus on doing that now instead of worrying about croaking it? We can expand our lifespan if we look after ourselves."

"Well, if you enjoy not eating junk food and exercising every day, go nuts. I'm going on a life adventure. I'm going to have fun resting my arse after years of toil, and eating whatever I want." That was Reg's philosophy on it all.

While this was a piss-take conversation, upon reflection, I'm not sure who's right: Reg's quest for adventure and fun, or my commitment to a healthy life so I can enjoy my grandkids? The best answer probably lies somewhere between both approaches.

Susan: I think you're right, Matt. I have friends who are obsessed with health routines to the point where it's sucking the life out of them and making them very serious.

Matt: Many of my friends are now focusing on how much time they have left – their survival based on superannuation and dealing with the rising cost of living. At the start of the second half, there's widespread anxiety about having the opportunity to enjoy the future. This anxiety is often made worse by government policies and the countless ads we see. In cultures where elders are valued, they are integrated into family responsibilities. They look after businesses, property and grandkids.

Susan: Our survey reinforced prior studies, showing that our happiness peaks in our early 20s, declines until it hits a low point between our mid-40s to mid-50s, then significantly elevates until we get close to 80. The drop in happiness after that is often due to dealing with ailments, or being put in homes where people feel isolated. So, how is this a helpful way to finish our book, Matt?

Matt: Well, we need to understand that life is finite; it doesn't matter whether you believe in an afterlife, or that this is your only shot. Embracing the uniqueness of the present moment and deciding how you want to **be**, is where it's at. If you focus on what you don't want, dwell on the negative or neglect self-care, you'll end up old, tired and grumpy, and that leads to sickness and a joyless life. It's your decision to see the goodness in yourself, in others and in this amazing planet we live on.

Susan: Yes, it's like that saying: *Choose your hard*. Self-care and discipline are hard, but so too is dealing with ill health.

Matt: I know that, particularly for men, the finite nature of life can often make us fear death. We dread the end of this amazing adventure, the thought of leaving our loved ones and causing distress. This reality should not elicit fear, but rather inspire us to embrace the joy, adventures and love that every moment can deliver. Great minds and prophets throughout human history have viewed the inevitability of death as a cue to fully embrace life.

Susan: I suppose Reg's point was this: do you have time to fully embrace life, if you are so busy following all your health routines?

Matt: I get it and, in this book, we have shared many tips. Even adopting just one will impact your life in positive ways. My hope is that people will take this information to develop their own life plan, tailor-made for them.

Susan: Love a plan! Where do we start?

Matt: Well, here are 10 questions everyone could ask themselves. The answers will help them develop a plan to seize the amazing opportunities life offers, and that each person truly deserves.

1. What brings me the most joy in my daily life? Identify the small and large activities or moments that consistently bring you happiness.
2. Who are the people that positively impact my life, and how can I nurture these relationships? Reflect on the significant relationships in your life and consider ways to strengthen them.
3. What are my core values, and how do they align with my daily actions and decisions? Examine whether your daily choices reflect your fundamental beliefs and principles.
4. How can I contribute to the wellbeing of others in my community and beyond? Consider the ways you can make a positive impact on others' lives, whether through volunteer work, acts of kindness, or professional contributions.
5. What are the physical activities that energise and rejuvenate me? Identify exercises or physical routines that not only keep you fit, but also uplift your spirit.
6. How do I currently manage stress, and what practices can I incorporate to enhance my mental and emotional wellbeing? Evaluate your current stress management techniques and explore additional methods such as meditation, mindfulness or hobbies.
7. What are the areas in my life where I feel unfulfilled, and what steps can I take to address them? Reflect on aspects of your life that may lack satisfaction and consider actionable steps to improve them.
8. How can I cultivate a sense of gratitude in my everyday life? Develop a daily gratitude practice, to focus on the positive aspects of your life.

9. What steps can I take to align my spiritual beliefs with my daily actions? Ensure that your actions reflect your spiritual values, whether through prayer, meditation or other spiritual practices.
10. How can I better appreciate and celebrate the present moment, rather than dwelling on the past or worrying about the future? Practise mindfulness and learn to savour the present, recognising that each moment is unique and valuable.

Susan: I like those. Even just reflecting on those questions would make a huge difference.

Matt: Then for the planners among us, I would recommend a few steps:

- **Self-Reflection**: Regularly take time to reflect on your answers to the questions above. Journaling can be a helpful tool for this process.

- **Set Intentional Goals**: Based on your reflections, set specific and achievable goals that align with your values and desires.

- **Create a Daily Routine**: Incorporate activities and practices into your daily routine that support your mental, physical, emotional and spiritual wellbeing.

- **Seek Support**: Engage with friends, family, or a professional coach or therapist to support your journey and provide accountability.

- **Celebrate Progress**: Acknowledge and celebrate the small victories and milestones along the way. This reinforces positive behaviour and keeps you motivated.
- **Adjust as Needed**: Life is dynamic, and your plan should be too. Be open to adjusting your goals and practices as you grow and change.

This approach and set of questions can help guide readers to a more fulfilling way of living. Embracing a holistic approach to life allows us to appreciate the richness of each moment and the interconnectedness of our experiences. You can revisit this resource and integrate more new approaches into the life you want.

I encourage everyone to choose happiness, vibrancy, love and gratitude, even though it's often harder than the alternatives. Ultimately, it's your choice to shape the life you desire.

Susan: Couldn't agree more, Matt. Hey, did you notice that we agreed on more things in this book than we disagreed on? Maybe men and women don't come from 2 different planets after all!

Appendix 1

Common symptoms of menopause may include:

Taken from www.jeanhailes.org.au

- *irregular periods*
- *hot flushes*
- *night sweats*
- *joint aches and pains*
- *sore breasts*
- *itchy, crawly or dry skin*
- *exhaustion and fatigue*
- *dry vagina*
- *loss of sex drive (libido)*
- *headache or migraine*
- *more intense premenstrual syndrome (PMS)*
- *sleep problems*
- *bloating*
- *urinary problems*
- *weight gain*

- *feeling irritable or frustrated*
- *feeling anxious*
- *difficulty concentrating*
- *brain fog*
- *forgetfulness*
- *lowered mood*
- *mood changes*
- *feeling you can't cope as well as you used to*

Recommended reading on menopause:

Dr Mary Claire Haver *The New Menopause: Navigating Your Path Through Hormonal Change with Purpose, Power and the Facts.* 2024, Rodale Books

Lisa Mosconi PhD *The Menopause Brain: New Science Empowers Women to Navigate the Pivotal Transition with Knowledge and Confidence.* 2024, Allen & Unwin

Dr Louise Newson *The Definitive Guide to the Perimenopause and Menopause.* 2023, Hodder & Stoughton

References

This book quotes a survey conducted by Susan and Matt in late 2024, which found that 47.38 percent of people were surviving, not thriving, in the second half. Only 47.01 percent of men reported they are thriving, compared to 57.95 percent of women. Results can be found at www.winningthesecondhalf.com

1. Levy, BR, Slade, MD, Kunkel, SR, Kasl, SV. Longevity increased by positive self-perceptions of aging. *J Pers Soc Psychol.* 2002 Aug;83(2):261-70.

2. An Australian survey conducted by Susan and Matt in late 2024 found that 47.38% of people were surviving not thriving in the second half. Only 47.01% of men reported they are thriving, compared to 57.95% of women. Results can be found at: https://www.winningthesecondhalf.com

3. Rauch, J. *The happiness curve: Why life gets better after 50.* 2018, Macmillan USA.

4. Dyer, Dr Wayne. *The Shift: Taking Your Life from Ambition to Meaning.* 2010, Hay House Australia.

5. Mosconi, L, Berti, V, Dyke, J et al. Menopause impacts human brain structure, connectivity, energy metabolism, and amyloid-beta deposition. *Sci Rep* 11, 10867 (2021).

6. Chatmon, BN. Males and Mental Health Stigma. *Am J Mens Health.* 2020, Jul-Aug;14(4):1557988320949322. PMID: 32812501; PMCID: PMC7444121.

7. *Bartley, EJ, Fillingim, RB. Sex differences in pain: a brief review of clinical and experimental findings. Br J Anaesth. 2013, Jul;111(1):52-8. doi: 10.1093/bja/aet127. PMID: 23794645; PMCID: PMC3690315.*

8. *Badawy, Y, Spector, A, Li, Z, Desai, R. The risk of depression in the menopausal stages: A systematic review and meta-analysis. J Affect Disord. 2024 Jul 15, 357:126-133. doi: 10.1016/j.jad.2024.04.041. Epub 2024 Apr 18. PMID: 38642901.*

9. *Ingalhalikar, M, Smith, A, Parker, D et al. (2013). Sex differences in the structural connectome of the human brain. Proceedings of the National Academy of Sciences USA. 111(2) 823-828. doi: 10.1073/pnas.1316909110.*

10. *Goyal, MS, Blazey, TM, Su, Y et al. (2019). Persistent metabolic youth in the aging female brain. Proceedings of the National Academy of Sciences USA. 116(8):3251-3255. doi: 10.1073/pnas.1815917116.*

11. *Ingalhalikar, M, Smith, A, Parker, D et al. (2013). Sex differences in the structural connectome of the human brain. Proceedings of the National Academy of Sciences USA. 111(2) 823-828. doi: 10.1073/pnas.1316909110.*

12. *National Academies of Sciences, Engineering and Medicine. (2020). Social Isolation and Loneliness in Older Adults: Opportunities for the Health Care System. Washington, DC: The National Academies Press. https://doi.org/10.17226/25663.*

13. *Stavrova, O, Fetchenhauer, D, Schlösser, T. (2013). Why are religious people happy? The effect of the social norm of religiosity across countries. Soc Sci Res. 2013 Jan; 42(1):90-105. doi: 10.1016/j.ssresearch.2012.07.002. Epub 2012 Jul 25. PMID: 23146600.*

14. *Lindqvist, E, Östling, R, Cesarini, D. (2020).* Long-Run Effects of Lottery Wealth on Psychological Well-Being, The Review of Economic Studies, 87(6): 2703-2726.

15. *Gur, RC, Turetsky, BI, Matsui, M et al. (1999). Sex differences in brain gray and white matter in healthy young adults: correlations with cognitive performance. J Neurosci. 1999 May 15; 19(10):4065-72. doi: 10.1523/JNEUROSCI.19-10-04065.*

About the Authors

Matt Elliott

With 18 years of experience as Head Coach in the NRL and UK Super League, Matt Elliott relentlessly pursued ways to merge wellbeing with high performance for his teams. However, while he was deeply committed to the success and welfare of others, his lack of personal self-care and unprocessed heartbreak led to an autoimmune disease called polymyalgia rheumatica (PMR), disconnecting him from the life and people he loved.

Recognising that his limited understanding of mental health was restricting his own wellbeing, Matt embarked on a journey to not only overcome his condition but to transform it into a catalyst for growth. By integrating his expertise in high performance with cutting-edge science on mental, physical and emotional health, he not only regained his vitality but also founded The Change Room, a nationally award-winning mental health and wellbeing initiative. This program has positively impacted tens of thousands of lives, helping individuals return to a functional, fulfilling life, while also supporting businesses and government agencies in reducing injury and enhancing productivity. He has gone on to create the BodySet Method.

As a bestselling author, radio commentator, and sought-after public speaker, Matt continues to explore the keys to longevity and thriving with joy. His mission is not just to help others perform at their best, but to ensure he can keep playing, learning and laughing with his grandkids for as long as possible.

More information on Matt and access to his international bestselling book, *The Change Room: Play the Game of Your Life*, is available at:

www.mattelliottcoach.com.au
and
www.thechangeroom.info

Susan Pearse

Susan Pearse is a bestselling author, speaker, and founder of Reinvention, recognised for her expertise in attention management and conscious leadership. With over 2 decades of experience, she has written 4 acclaimed books and is a sought-after keynote speaker. Her insights have been featured across TV, podcasts, magazines, news sites and documentaries.

A quarter-life crisis, a shopping trip to New York, and a chance meeting with His Holiness the Dalai Lama led to the discovery of her life's purpose: to wake up the world. Susan swapped clothes shopping for wisdom shopping, exploring everything from quantum physics and neuroscience to crystals and chakras. And Susan found one core truth that she now teaches people in all walks of life: the need to get out of your head, into your body and fully connect with your life.

Passionate about fostering entrepreneurial and adaptive thinking, Susan guest lectures at universities and helps individuals and organisations embrace new ways of working and leading.

Based in Queensland, Australia, she finds inspiration by the ocean, often writing by the water where her best ideas emerge. This latest book continues her mission to help readers cultivate fulfilment and presence in both their personal and professional lives.

Learn more at: www.susanpearse.com

Other books by Susan Pearse:

- *Wired for Life: Retrain Your Brain and Thrive* (Hay House)
- *One Moment Please: It's Time to Pay Attention* (Hay House)
- *Do Less Be More: Ban Busy and Make Space for What Matters* (Hay House)
- *Spiritually Loose: Uncover the Path to Your Divine Life* (Hay House)

About Some of Matt and Susan's Influences

There are 3 inspiring individuals who have profoundly influenced the physical section's approach to wellbeing. These mentors, along with numerous other experts, have shaped the content in Section 4:

Anthony Minichiello: A former professional rugby league player, Mini's journey from repeated back injuries to a revitalised state using the Weston A Price diet and functional exercise is nothing short of remarkable. His insights, honed over 14 years, are now recognised as cutting edge by experts worldwide.

Dr Mark Hyman: A beacon of common sense merged with cutting-edge science, Dr Hyman's approach to making health knowledge applicable in daily life is unparalleled. Dive into his podcasts and books like *Food Fix* and *Young Forever* for a transformative experience.

Nam Baldwin: Introduced to Matt by world surfing champion, Mick Fanning, Nam's focus on breathing's impact on performance and wellbeing was ahead of its time. His work with elite athletes and individuals alike has showcased the profound effects of mindful breathing.

www.ingramcontent.com/pod-product-compliance
Lightning Source LLC
Chambersburg PA
CBHW061228070526
44584CB00030B/4039